WORLD OF READING

WORKBOOK

·GOING· PLACES

P. David Pearson   Dale D. Johnson

Theodore Clymer   Roselmina Indrisano   Richard L. Venezky

James F. Baumann   Elfrieda Hiebert   Marian Toth

Consulting Authors

Carl Grant   Jeanne Paratore

SILVER BURDETT & GINN

NEEDHAM, MA • MORRISTOWN, NJ

ATLANTA, GA • CINCINNATI, OH • DALLAS, TX

MENLO PARK, CA • NORTHFIELD, IL

Illustration Credits

Janet Bohn, pp. 19, 36, 58, 59, 62, 69; Randy Chewning, pp. 15, 18, 28, 87; Daniel Delvalle, pp. 14, 27, 32, 64, 65, 71, 90, 135; Eldon Doty, pp. 37, 43, 46. 51, 72, 76, 91, 106, 107, 110, 115, 117, 129, 155; Leslie Dunlop, pp. 8, 29, 147, 153; Meryl Henderson, pp. 47, 63, 88, 105, 132, 159; Brian Karas, pp. 7, 31, 48, 50, 52, 56, 75, 85, 94, 96, 98, 113, 130, 140, 151, 158, 161; Jane Kendall, p. 149; Linda Knox, pp. 77-79, 100, 104; Dora Leder, pp. 142, 143; N. Jo Lenard, p. 10; Ben Mahan, pp. 127, 134, 136, 146; Sal Murdocca, pp. 5, 6, 9, 13, 17, 44, 45, 49, 53-55, 68, 86, 89, 112, 128, 131, 138, 150, 157, 160; Sandy Rabinowitz, p. 114; David Rickman, p. 33; Dixon Scott, pp. 16, 26, 34, 35, 60, 61, 70, 74, 97, 102, 103, 118, 121, 133, 139, 141; Arvis Stewart, pp. 119, 120; Freya Tanz, pp. 12, 20-23, 30, 57, 92, 95, 99, 116, 137, 148, 152, 154; Barbara Todd, pp. 93, 101; George Ulrich, pp. 11, 156.

ISBN 0-663-46175-8

TABLE OF CONTENTS

TABLE OF CONTENTS

What Interests Me

Circle the pictures that show things you like to read about.
Use the chart to find out which books you would enjoy.

1	2	3	4	BOOK LIST
	★	★	★	*Best Friends for Frances* by Russell Hoban
★		★	★	*Dabble Duck* by Anne Leo Ellis
★		★		*Alexander and the Wind-Up Mouse* by Leo Lionni
	★		★	*Friends* by Helme Heine
★	★			*A Porcupine Named Fluffy* by Helen Lester

NAME _____

My Book List

Name of Book

_____
- -
_____

Author

_____
- -
_____

Name of Book

_____
- -
_____

Author

_____
- -
_____

Story Mapping

> **REMEMBER:** A **story map** tells the beginning, middle, and ending of a story.

A. Write the words to finish the story map.

| Amy   happy   sad |

A Letter to Amy

Beginning:
Who
Where
When

_____

Peter wanted _____ to come to a party at his house. It was on Saturday. So he wrote her a letter.

Middle:
Problem

When Peter ran to mail the letter, the wind blew it away. Peter chased the letter and bumped right into

_____

Amy. She was not happy. Peter was _____ because he was sure Amy would not come to the party.

To Peter's surprise, Amy came. And she brought with

_____

her a parrot. It wished Peter a _____ birthday!

B. On another paper, write Peter's thank-you note to Amy.

Words with *ou, ow (cloud, cow)*

> **REMEMBER:** The letters *ou* and *ow* can stand for the
> vowel sound you hear in *cloud* and *cow.*

A. Read each set of words. Circle the word that has the
vowel sound you hear in *cow.*

1. know   down   would
2. through   ground   grow
3. throw   thought   now
4. found   country   should

B. Use the words you circled in Part A to finish the sentences.

5. My friend Anna _____ a beautiful stone in the park.

6. It was just sitting on the _____ .

7. Anna put the stone _____ in my hand.

8. She said, ''The stone is yours _____ , Jen.''

C. Choose any two words you wrote in Part B. On another paper, write
each word in a sentence about two friends.

Using New Words

A. Write the words to finish the sentences.

greetings	laundromat	laundry bag	package	suitcase

1. The two socks met in the _____ .

place where people wash clothes

2. They had come there in a _____ .

sack that holds clothes to be washed

3. The red sock told the blue sock that he had been part of

a _____ of three pairs of red

socks.   thing wrapped or tied up

4. He said he had been all over the world. He traveled everywhere in

a _____ .

case used for clothes while traveling

5. The blue sock said, ''When I travel, I always send

_____ to my fellow socks.''

good wishes from someone not present

B. On another paper, write one more thing the socks might say to
one another. Use as many story words as you can.

NAME _____

Mitchell Is Moving

A. Write one or more words on each line to finish the story about "Mitchell Is Moving."

house   Margo   post card   stay   tired

Mitchell wanted to move. He was _____ of living

in the same old place. His friend, _____ , wanted him

to _____ . She said that she would glue Mitchell to the roof to keep him there.

Mitchell moved anyway. He moved to a place that was two weeks away. Each day as he moved, he sent Margo a

_____ . He liked his new home, but he missed Margo.

Mitchell wrote to Margo and asked her to come live near him.

Margo came, and she built a new _____ next to Mitchell's house.

The two friends were happy to be together again.

B. Pretend you are Mitchell. On another paper, write a post card to Margo.

Words with *ph*

> **REMEMBER:** The letters *ph* can stand for the sound you hear at the beginning of *photo*.

A. Write the word that makes sense in each sentence and has *ph* in it.

_____

1. Mitchell talked on the _____ to Margo.

                photo   phone   play

2. He said, "Margo, I have a new friend. He has a

   _____

   toy _____ ."

           photo   phase   elephant

3. "It is a very funny toy," said Mitchell. "I have

   _____

   taken a _____ of it."

           plate   phone   photo

4. Then Mitchell's friend talked to Margo on the

   _____

   _____ , too.

           family   photo   telephone

B. On another paper, draw a picture that shows what the toy looks like. Write a sentence that goes with your picture. Use words that have the letters *ph* that stand for the sound you hear at the beginning of *photo*.

NAME _____

Words with *ou, ow (cloud, cow)*

REMEMBER: The letters *ou* and *ow* can stand for the vowel sound in *cloud* and *cow*.

A. Write the words to finish the poem about what Mitchell and Margo saw.

| brown | cloud | down | hours |

Mitchell and Margo went to town,
And these are some of the things they found.
_____

A kite that went up, and one that came _____ .
_____

A cat that was black, and a dog that was _____ .
Bicycles quiet, and trucks that were loud.
In the park, some beautiful flowers.
_____

High in the sky, a big white _____ .
_____

And one tall clock that told the _____ .

B. On another paper, write two sentences about other things Mitchell and Margo might have seen in town. Use at least one word with *ou* or *ow* in your sentences.

Figurative Language

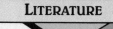

> **REMEMBER:** Writers may compare things that are alike in one way but different in every other way. This can help you see things in a new and exciting way.

A. Read each sentence. Then underline the sentence that tells you about Margo.

1. One day Margo sat at her desk, quiet as a mouse.
   a. Margo hid under her desk.
   b. Margo was very, very quiet.
   c. Margo made loud mouse noises.

2. Mitchell said, "You are as busy as a bee, Margo."
   a. Margo was very busy.
   b. Margo was taking care of bees.
   c. Margo was writing about bees.

3. Margo's smile was as bright as the sun. "I'm making a birthday card for you, Mitchell," she said.
   a. Margo's smile was very big and warm.
   b. Margo's smile was small and far away.
   c. Margo smiled all day long.

B. Think of another animal or thing that Margo was like as she worked. Then write a sentence about Margo on another paper.

Using New Words

A. Write the word to finish each sentence.

fastened	knots	newspaper
pencils	practice	probably

1. We read about the kite contest in the

_____

- -

_____ .

2. Denny and I got a form and filled it out with

_____

- -

our _____ .

3. After we mailed the form, Denny said, "We

_____

- -

_____ should get ready."

_____

- -

4. We _____ the tails to the kites.

_____

- -

5. Then we made good _____ .

_____

- -

6. Denny and I will _____ until we are

good enough to win the contest.

B. On another paper, write a sentence that tells how a kite

flies. Use *like* or *as* in your sentence.

Gloria

WHO MIGHT BE MY BEST FRIEND

A. Write one or more words on each line to finish the story about "Gloria Who Might Be My Best Friend."

Gloria	kite	same	secret wishes	wind

This story is about Julian. One day he met

_____

- -

a girl named _____ . Julian wanted

Gloria to be his friend.

Gloria showed Julian how to make

_____

- -

_____ . First they made a

_____

- - - - - - - - - - - - - - - - - - -

_____ . Then they wrote secret wishes on pieces of

paper and tied them to the tail of the kite.

They flew the kite. When they pulled the kite down, their paper

_____

- - - - - - - - - - - - -

wishes were gone. Gloria said the _____ had taken them.

Julian asked Gloria if she had wished that they would be friends.

Gloria would not tell, but Julian was sure they had made the

_____

- - - - - - - - - - - - - -

_____ wish.

B. Do you think Julian and Gloria's wishes will come true? Write two sentences about what you think on another paper.

NAME

Words with *ie*

REMEMBER: The letters *ie* can stand for the vowel sound you hear in *field*.

A. Write the word that makes sense in each sentence.

1. Gloria and Julian sat together and talked in a

_____

_ _ _ _ _ _ _ _ _ _ _ _ _ _ _ _ _ _ _

_____ of grass.

   brief   field   science

2. Gloria told Julian, "I wish I could visit beautiful

_____

_ _ _ _ _ _ _ _ _ _ _ _ _ _ _ _ _ _

_____ made of gold."

   parties   times   cities

3. Julian said, "I wish I could meet

_____

_ _ _ _ _ _ _ _ _ _ _ _ _ _ _ _ _ _

_____ Longears.

   Chief   Mister   Shield

_____

_ _ _ _ _ _ _ _ _ _ _ _ _ _ _ _ _ _

4. "And I wish I had a _____ of apple to eat,"
said Gloria.   piece   relief   quiet

B. On another paper, write a sentence that tells about a wish you would like to make.

Figurative Language

> **REMEMBER:** Writers may compare things that are alike in one way but different in every other way. This can help you see things in a new and exciting way.

A. Circle the word that belongs in each sentence. Then write the word on the line.

1. Like a _____ , the kite flew higher and higher.

   stone   bird   flower

2. Julian stood, still as a _____ , watching it.

   stone   bird   ant

3. The kite danced in the clouds like a _____ .

   butterfly   lamp   stone

4. Then the kite floated down like a_____ .

   clown   tree   snowflake

5. Julian raced like a _____ to the kite.

   stone   deer   flower

B. Choose one sentence in Part A. On another paper, tell why you picked the word you did to finish the sentence.

NAME _____

Drawing Conclusions

> **REMEMBER:** When you draw a **conclusion,** you figure
> out things that are not explained in a story. Use story
> clues and what you already know to draw a conclusion.

A. Read each story. Then answer the questions.

1. The moon was beginning to rise. Julian said, "It's late. I have
   to go home, Gloria."

   _____

   _____

   What time of day was it? _____

2. The park was quiet. Julian and Gloria rushed along through the
   snow. They wanted to get inside the house where it was warm.

   _____

   _____

   What time of year was it? _____

3. Julian's book and colored pencils were missing. He went to his
   little sister's room. He saw his pencils on the rug. His book
   was there, too.

   Who had taken Julian's book and colored pencils?

   _____

   _____

   _____

B. Think of a place where you do special things. On
   another paper, write about the things you do there
   without telling what the place is.

Using New Words

A. Read the word in the circle. Then read the word
meanings. Write the word that matches each meaning.

| argued | break | bundle | gathered | group | sons |

_____   _____

things or people that   boy children
are together

(together)

_____   _____

brought together   things tied together

B. Write words from the box to match the meanings.

_____   _____

disagreed   snap into pieces

C. On another paper, write three sentences about a family
that worked together to make something. Use as many
story words as you can.

The Bundle of Sticks

A. Write one or more words on each line to finish the story about "The Bundle of Sticks."

bundle of sticks	fence	sons	strong	together

_____

This story is about three _____ who lived on a farm. They

argued about which one could build the best _____ .

That made the father very sad. He said that they should work

_____

_____ , but they would not. So the father

decided to teach them a lesson.

He gave each son a stick and asked him to break it. Each one did this easily. Then he asked them to break a

_____

_____ .

None of them could do this.

The sons understood the lesson. Sticks—and people—are weak by themselves. Sticks put together in a bundle are

_____

_____—so are people who work together.

B. On another paper, write about some other job that the sons did on the farm. Tell why it was easier to finish the job when the sons worked together.

Words with *u*

> **REMEMBER:** The letter *u* can stand for the vowel sound
> you hear in *put*.

A. Read each sentence. Circle the two words in which the
letter *u* stands for the vowel sound you hear in *put*.
Then write the words on the lines.

1. The brothers went outside to put the bull back in the barn.

_____   _____

_____   _____

2. But when Peter pulled, it just sat down in the bushes.

_____   _____

_____   _____

3. The brothers found a way. Peter pulled while John and David pushed.

_____   _____

_____   _____

4. It took a full hour, but they got the bull back into the barn.

_____   _____

_____   _____

B. On another paper, write a sentence about the bull once
it was in the barn. Use one word in which the letter *u*
stands for the vowel sound you hear in *put*.

NAME _____

Drawing Conclusions

> **REMEMBER:** When you draw a **conclusion,** you figure out things that are not explained in a story. Use story clues and what you already know to draw a conclusion.

A. Read each story. Then write the answers.

1. "Wake up, John!" said Father. "You will have to go out and dig a path through the snow to the barn. Then please feed the cows."

This story took place on a _____ .

The time of day was _____ .

The time of year was _____ .

2. Peter sat at the table. His mother was standing by the stove. She asked, "What would you like for lunch, Peter?" Peter said, "I would like to have an egg sandwich."

What time of day was it? _____

In what room was Peter sitting? _____

B. Read story 1 again. How did you know where the story took took place? Change the story so that it takes place in a city. Write your new story on another paper.

Words with *ou, ow (cloud, cow)*

> **REMEMBER:** The letters *ou* and *ow* can stand for the
> vowel sound in *cloud* and *cow.*

A. Write the words to finish the poem.

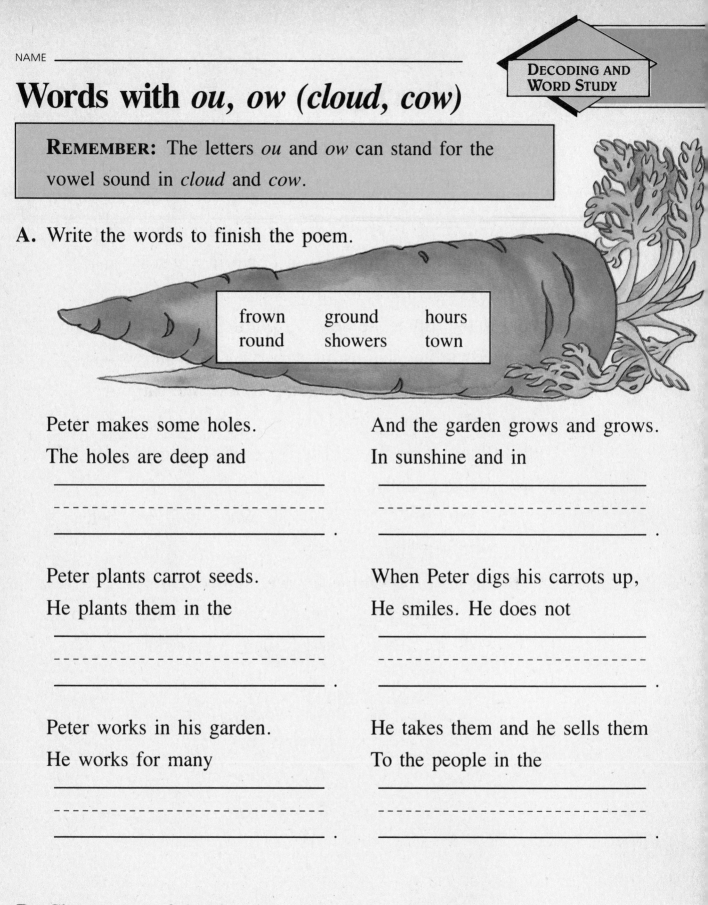

frown	ground	hours
round	showers	town

Peter makes some holes.
The holes are deep and

_____

_____ .

And the garden grows and grows.
In sunshine and in

_____

_____ .

Peter plants carrot seeds.
He plants them in the

_____

_____ .

When Peter digs his carrots up,
He smiles. He does not

_____

_____ .

Peter works in his garden.
He works for many

_____

_____ .

He takes them and he sells them
To the people in the

_____

_____ .

B. Choose two of the rhyming words you wrote. On
another paper, write a two-line poem using those words.

Checkpoint

Read the story. Then fill in the circle next to the correct answer.

One morning I went to school. I walked through my town as quick as a bunny. I sat down in my seat, just as I always do. But something was different about school today. Someone new was sitting next to me!

She sat in her seat as quiet as a mouse. She was quiet all during math and reading times. She sat and frowned all morning long. I wished she wouldn't be so sad. At lunch time I would try to cheer her up. I would be as silly as a clown.

"I'm hungry," I said out loud when the lunch bell rang. "Are you hungry, too?"

The new girl looked at me and smiled. She said, "Yes! I'm as hungry as a bear." We walked together to the crowded lunch room, and I knew we would be friends.

1. In the story, the words *as quick as a bunny* mean the person walked to school ___ .
- (a) all alone
- (b) fast
- (c) by jumping like a bunny

2. In the story, the words *as quiet as a mouse* tell you that the new girl ___ .
- (a) did not do her work
- (b) did not listen
- (c) did not talk

3. Which sentence helped you know what *as quiet as a mouse* means?
- (a) She was quiet all during math and reading times.
- (b) She sat and frowned all morning long.
- (c) The new girl looked at me.

4. In the story, the words *as hungry as a bear* mean the new girl ___ .
- (a) wanted to eat a bear
- (b) was very hungry
- (c) looked like a bear

5. Which word has the same vowel sound as the underlined letters in *cl<u>ou</u>d*?
- (a) cone
- (b) could
- (c) clown
- (d) cut

6. Which word has the same vowel sound as the underlined letters in *c<u>ow</u>*?
- (a) mouse
- (b) mat
- (c) move
- (d) mow

7. Which word has the same vowel sound as the underlined letters in *h<u>ou</u>se*?
- (a) flow
- (b) frowned
- (c) four
- (d) fox

8. Which word has the same vowel sound as the underlined letters in *cl<u>ou</u>d*?
- (a) crook
- (b) could
- (c) crop
- (d) crowded

NAME _____

Words with r-Controlled Vowels

REMEMBER: When the letter *r* comes after a vowel letter or letters, the *r* makes a difference in the vowel sound.

A. Write the word that makes sense in the sentence and has the vowel sound you hear in *learn*, *her*, *first*, and *fur*.

_____

1. The sons could _____ money by doing extra work.

   easy
   earn

2. Their father asked them to build a house for

   the _____ .

   birds
   boards

3. The _____ thing they did was put some pieces of wood together.

   fist
   first

4. Then they made a _____ for the birds to sit on.

   peach
   perch

5. They made the roof _____ to keep out the rain.

   carve
   curve

B. On another paper, write two sentences about the birdhouse the the sons built. Use two words with the *r*-controlled vowel sound.

Using New Words

A. Write the word that means the same or almost the same as the underlined word or words.

ax	breathe	chimney	dirt	hammer	stitches	tiny

1. I'm going to make a <u>little</u> house. _____

2. The <u>tool used to chop</u> can cut trees. _____

3. I'll <u>use a tool to nail</u> the wood together. _____

4. With windows I can <u>take in and out</u> the fresh
air. _____

5. I'll sew <u>threads going in and out</u>
on my curtains. _____

6. I'll make a <u>stone opening</u> in my roof. _____

7. My house will have a <u>soil</u> floor. _____

B. On another paper, write two sentences about building your own house. Use as many story words as you can.

Tony's Hard Work Day

A. Write one or more words on each line to finish the story
about "Tony's Hard Work Day."

built a house	country	Tony	Tony's house	too small

This story is about a boy named _____ .

His family bought a house in the _____ .

The house needed a lot of work. But no one in the family would
let Tony help fix up the house. Tony's father said he
_____

was _____ to hammer. His brother sent him
off to play.

Tony went off by himself and _____
of his own. When the house was finished, his father, his mother, and
his two brothers said it looked like a good place to live. The family
_____

moved right into _____ and stayed forever.

B. Fold another paper in half. On one side, draw the house
Tony's family bought in the country. On the other side,
draw Tony's house. Write a sentence telling which house
you would like to move into and why.

Following Directions

> **REMEMBER: Directions** are steps for doing something. When following directions, read or listen carefully, do the steps in the correct order, and don't skip any steps.

A. Here are directions for building a house just like Tony's. Write the best direction word to finish each sentence.

Chop	Dig	Lay	Fill	Weave	Tie

1. _____ a big hole in the ground.

2. _____ the hole with stones for a floor.

3. _____ down trees for walls.

4. _____ one log on top of the other to make walls.

5. _____ some trees together with vines for a roof.

6. _____ a rug for the floor.

B. On another paper, draw a picture of the house in Part A. Write two sentences that tell about your picture.

NAME _____

Words with *r*-Controlled Vowels

> **REMEMBER:** When the letter *r* comes after a vowel letter or letters, the *r* can make a difference in the vowel sound.

A. Read each set of words. Circle the word that has the vowel sound you hear in *her, first, fur,* or *learn.*

1. true   tired   turned

2. herd   hard   here

3. fir   fire   for

4. ear   pear   early

B. Use the words you circled in Part A to finish the sentences.

5. Tony's house had _____ trees all around it.

6. Then Tony _____ the land into a farm.

7. He kept a _____ of cows in a barn he built.

8. _____ each morning, Tony's rooster woke up all the people.

C. On another paper, write two sentences about Tony's farm. Use as many words as you can that have the sound you hear in the middle of *learn.*

Drawing Conclusions

> **REMEMBER:** When you draw a **conclusion,** you figure out things that are not explained in a story. Use story clues and what you already know to draw a conclusion.

A. Write the word or words to finish each story.

1. The sun was out. There was lots of green grass. Flowers were _____ everywhere. It was _____ .

snowy   warm   cold

2. Tony wanted to help. His father wouldn't let him hammer. His mother wouldn't let him sew curtains. His brother wouldn't _____ let him paint. Tony felt _____ .

sad   happy   afraid

3. Tony worked hard all morning. He found lots of stones. He chopped down trees. He was very hungry. Tony was ready _____ to _____ .

go to sleep   go to work   eat lunch

B. What conclusion can you draw about Tony's not being able to help his family fix up the house? On another paper, write a sentence about what you think.

NAME

Comparison

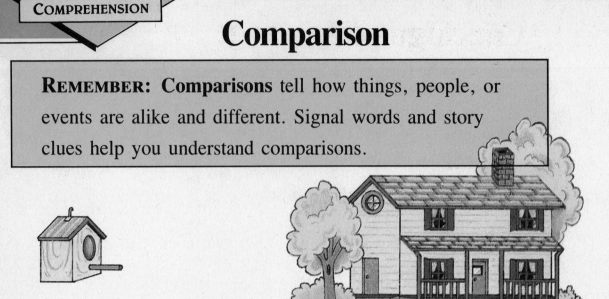

> **REMEMBER: Comparisons** tell how things, people, or events are alike and different. Signal words and story clues help you understand comparisons.

A. Look at the two houses. Circle **alike** if the sentence tells a way that Tony's house is like the birdhouse. Circle **different** if it tells a way they are different.

1. Tony's house is not tiny.   alike   different

2. Tony's house is made of wood.   alike   different

3. Tony's house has a chimney.   alike   different

4. Tony's house has a roof.   alike   different

5. Tony's house has a way to go in.   alike   different

6. Tony's house has curtains.   alike   different

7. Tony's house has a porch.   alike   different

B. On another paper, draw a house that is different from each of these houses. Write a sentence that tells one way it is different from the birdhouse. Write a sentence that tells one way it is the same as Tony's house.

Using New Words

A. Write the words to finish the story.

ambulance	bump	hospital	neighbor	yesterday

My grandmother called us on the phone
_____
_____ .

She said my grandfather fell and got a
_____
_____ on his head. She called

_____

a next-door _____ for help.

_____

An _____ came to get my

_____

grandfather. He went to the _____ .

My grandmother said that he will be fine. She was glad there was
someone to help her.

B. Think of a story about a person or animal who needs
help. On another paper, write three sentences telling
what happens.

NAME _____

A Special Trade

A. Write one or more words on each line to finish the story about "A Special Trade."

| Bartholomew "ham and eggs" Nelly special trade wheelchair |

This story is about two neighbors who were very special friends.

_____

When _____ was small, her friend Bartholomew would take her for walks. All the neighbors called them

_____

_____ because they were always together.

Nelly and Bartholomew both grew older. One day,

_____

_____ fell and couldn't

walk anymore. Bartholomew thought their walking days were over, but Nelly had another idea. Now she could push Bartholomew through the

_____

streets in his _____ .

Now it was Bartholomew's turn to be pushed, as he used to do for

_____

her. It was a kind of _____ .

B. Can two people who are very different be good friends? On another paper, tell why or why not in two or three sentences.

NAME _____

Long Word Decoding

> **REMEMBER:** When you try to read a long word, look for words and word parts you know.

A. Circle the words or word parts you know. Underline the vowel letters.

final   footsteps   cabin   sprinkled   toaster

B. Write one of the words in Part A to answer each question.

1. One meaning of this word is "rained lightly." Which word is it? _____

2. Which word means the opposite of *first*? _____

3. Which word names something often used with bread? _____

4. Which word means "a small wooden house"? _____

5. Which word names something you make as you walk? _____

C. On another paper, use two of the words you wrote in Part B to write a sentence of your own.

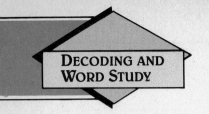

NAME _____

Words with *r*-Controlled Vowels

REMEMBER: When the letter *r* comes after a vowel letter or letters, the *r* makes a difference in the vowel sound.

A. Read the story. Circle the words that have an *r* that makes a difference in the vowel sound. Then write the words in the chart.

One day, Nelly's friend fell and got hurt. At first, he felt like a sad bird. He thought he might burst into tears. Oh, how he missed his walks with Nelly. But Nelly knew it was her turn to help him. She could be his nurse. She learned to push his wheelchair along the curb. Sometimes she would serve him lemonade.

er	ir	ur	ear

B. On another paper, write three sentences about friends helping each other. Use one of the words you wrote in Part A in each sentence.

36 *"A Special Trade"*   *r*-Controlled Vowels

Figurative Language

> **REMEMBER:** Writers may compare things that are alike in one way but different in every other way. This can help you see things in a new and exciting way.

A. Read each sentence. Underline the people, animals, or things that are compared.

1. Nelly and Bartholomew were like ham and eggs.

2. They took lots of walks and kept as busy as bees.

3. Sometimes they liked to sit on the porch and be as quiet as mice.

4. Sometimes Bartholomew would make his harmonica sing like a bird.

5. One day Nelly was as hungry as a bear.

6. She ran like a deer to the store.

7. Nelly was back as quick as a wink.

8. She sat down on the porch like a tired dog.

B. On another paper, draw picture of a tired dog. Then draw another picture that shows Nelly sitting on the porch in a way that is like the tired dog. Write a sentence of your own to go with your second picture.

Checkpoint

Read the story. Then fill in the circle next to the correct answer.

It was Saturday. Gert and her best friend Pearl were planning a special day together. They would have lots of fun. Gert waited for Pearl on her porch. Each girl had her lunch in her purse.

Off they went. They took turns pushing each other on the swings. Gert's turn was first. Then they took a walk. They looked at ferns and flowers. The girls looked for a good place to eat their lunch. They didn't want to sit in the dirt. Pearl found a place under a fir tree. The girls took out their forks and ate their food.

Suddenly, Gert and Pearl heard a very loud sound in the sky. The friends knew they had to hurry home. They picked up their things and ran home as fast as they could, laughing all the way!

NAME _____

1. Where did Gert and Pearl go?
   (a) to a farm
   (b) to the city
   (c) to the park

2. Why did Gert and Pearl have to hurry home?
   (a) They were going to get wet.
   (b) They were hungry.
   (c) They were going to be late.

3. Which sentence in the story helped you know why they had to hurry home?
   (a) Pearl found a place under a fir tree.
   (b) Suddenly, Gert and Pearl heard a very loud sound in the sky.
   (c) Each girl had her lunch in her purse.

4. Which word has the same vowel sound as the underlined letters in *bird*?
   (a) fire   (c) far
   (b) fur   (d) fun

5. Which word has the same vowel sound as the underlined letters in *her*?
   (a) hurt   (c) here
   (b) hear   (d) hen

6. Which word has the same vowel sound as the underlined letters in *fur*?
   (a) east   (c) eat
   (b) ear   (d) early

7. Which word has the same vowel sound as the underlined letters in *fir*?
   (a) fort   (c) fern
   (b) far   (d) fear

8. Which word has the same vowel sound as the underlined letters in *learn*?
   (a) peach   (c) punch
   (b) perch   (d) pear

Vocabulary Review

Fill in the circle next to the word that best fits in the sentence.

1. The ___ in our school is next to my classroom.
   ⓐ sons ⓑ gym ⓒ suitcase ⓓ neighbor

2. An ant is a ___ bug.
   ⓐ giant ⓑ public ⓒ tiny ⓓ famous

3. In the ___ , Dad cut down a tree.
   ⓐ ax ⓑ sons ⓒ package ⓓ forest

4. Use this ___ to chop the wood.
   ⓐ bundle ⓑ ax ⓒ pencils ⓓ newspaper

5. Sharon took a ___ of clothes to be washed.
   ⓐ dirt ⓑ ambulance ⓒ bundle ⓓ taste

6. Jennifer ___ a pin to her new coat.
   ⓐ breathe ⓑ fastened ⓒ hammer ⓓ argued

7. Jim tied two ___ in the rope.
   ⓐ knots ⓑ greetings ⓒ stitches ⓓ group

8. Sara rode her bike over a ___ in the road.

(a) yesterday   (b) bump   (c) pepper   (d) chimney

9. That glass will ___ if you drop it.

(a) break   (b) breathe   (c) practice   (d) gathered

10. You can ___ through your nose or your mouth.

(a) break   (b) fastened   (c) enter   (d) breathe

11. The children ___ their books and went to school.

(a) break   (b) gathered   (c) breathe   (d) enter

12. A ___ is a place where doctors work.

(a) bundle   (b) laundromat   (c) hospital   (d) pencils

13. A ___ tells you about things that have happened.

(a) bump   (b) newspaper   (c) bundle   (d) taste

14. My ___ took care of my dog when I went away.

(a) ax   (b) knots   (c) pencils   (d) neighbor

15. Tina used her colored ___ to draw that picture.

(a) hammer   (b) knots   (c) pencils   (d) chimney

NAME —————————————————————

Unit Wrap-Up

Write the answer to each question.

1. In "The Bundle of Sticks," the sons worked together to make a fence. In "Gloria Who Might Be My Best Friend," what did Gloria and Julian make together?

2. In "Tony's Hard Work Day," Tony helped his family by building a house. How did Nelly help Bartholomew in "A Special Trade"?

3. In what way were Bartholomew and Nelly like Julian and Gloria? In what way were they different?

What Interests Me

Circle the pictures that show things you like to read about.
Use the chart to find out which books you would enjoy.

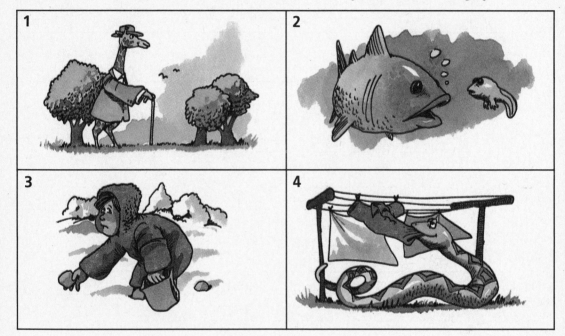

1	2	3	4	BOOK LIST
★			★	*A Giraffe and a Half* by Shel Silverstein
★	★			*Fish Is Fish* by Leo Lionni
		★	★	*Crictor* by Tomi Ungerer
	★	★		*Annie and the Wild Animals* by Jan Brett
		★	★	*The Day Jimmy's Boa Ate the Wash* by Trinka Hakes Noble

NAME _____

My Book List

Name of Book

_____

- -

_____

Author

_____

- -

_____

Name of Book

_____

- -

_____

Author

_____

- -

_____

Antonyms

> **REMEMBER: Antonyms** are words that have opposite
> or nearly opposite meanings. *Stop* and *go* are antonyms.
> *Tall* and *short* are also antonyms.

A. Read each pair of sentences. Write the antonym for the
underlined word.

awake	brave	dry	safe	tame

1. The big lion was not <u>afraid</u> of anything. He was _____ .

2. Sheep and cows once were <u>wild</u> animals. Today they are
   _____ .

3. After the bear cub fell into the pond, he was all <u>wet</u>. He
   sat in the sun, and soon he was _____ .

4. The rabbit was <u>asleep</u> in his bed, until the wolf howled.
   Then she was wide _____ .

5. Beth's father thought that the raccoon was <u>dangerous</u>.
   Her mother said that it was _____ for Beth to keep.

B. On another paper, write two sentences about a wild
animal. In the second sentence, use an antonym for a
word in the first sentence.

NAME _____

Main Idea/Details

REMEMBER: The **main idea** is the most important idea in a paragraph. Supporting details tell more about the main idea.

A. Read each paragraph. Write the sentence that tells the main idea.

1. Everybody likes to read stories. Some people like to read about animals. Some people like to read about people doing things that are fun.

_____

- -

_____

2. Some stories are about real people. Some tell about real places that you can go. True stories tell about things that are real.

_____

- -

_____

_____

- -

_____

3. I like make-believe stories best. The stories can be about anything at all. Sometimes they tell about magic things.

_____

- -

_____

B. On another paper, write one more detail sentence to go with each of the main ideas in Part A.

Using New Words

A. Write the word that is opposite in meaning to the underlined word.

difficult	enemy	fact	fiction	loses	shoot

1. I have a good <u>friend</u>. _____

2. It is <u>easy</u> for us to find things to do. _____

3. Sometimes we read stories of <u>make-believe</u> together.

   _____

4. Sometimes we play school and teach each other <u>facts</u>.

   _____

5. When a person <u>finds</u> a good friend like mine, he or she is

   _____

   happy. _____

B. There is one word left. It means "send forth swiftly."

   _____

   What is the word? _____

C. Fold a piece of paper in half. On one side draw a picture of something make-believe. On the other side draw a picture of something real.

NAME _____

Animal Fact and Fiction

A. Write one or more words on each line to finish the story
about "Animal Fact and Fiction."

afraid   animals   fact   fiction   to protect themselves

This story tells both fact and fiction about some

_____

- -

_____ .

Ostriches really do not stick their heads in the sand. They drop down

_____

- -

and stretch out their necks when they are _____ .

Porcupines cannot really shoot their quills, but they do use them

_____

- -

_____ .

- -

It is a _____ that a special fish called the

mud skipper can climb branches in the water.

The story shows that it is important to tell fact from

_____

- -

_____ .

B. Think of something about an animal that is fact and something
that is fiction. On another paper, write a sentence about each.

Suffixes *-ful, -less*

REMEMBER: The suffix *-ful* means "full of." The suffix *-less* means "without."

A. Read the stories. Write a word to finish each story.

cheerful	fearless	forgetful	helpful

1. Is it true that an elephant never forgets? No, it is not. Like all

_____

animals, the elephant is sometimes _____ .

2. The tiger charges at its enemy. It shows no fear. The tiger is

_____

a _____ animal.

3. Many birds sing songs. They are full of good cheer. Many birds'

_____

songs are very _____ .

4. A certain kind of fish helps the shark to stay clean. The shark helps

_____

the fish find food. The two fish are _____
to each other.

B. Look at the word *care*. Make new words by adding the suffixes *-ful* and *-less*. On another paper, use the new words to write two sentences about an animal.

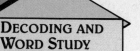

NAME _____

Words with Silent Letters

> **REMEMBER:** The letters *gn*, *kn*, and *wr* can stand for the sound you hear at the beginning of *gnaw*, *know*, and *write*.

A. Read the story. Circle all the words that begin with *gn*, *kn*, or *wr*. Then write the words in the chart.

    Everyone knows that dogs do not talk and cannot write. But we are wrong if we think that dogs do not tell us things. Dogs let their needs be known. Some can wreck a quiet night with their bark. They knock on the door by scratching. Some dogs gnaw at things when they feel like playing.

kn	wr	gn

B. On another paper, draw a picture that shows what a dog can do when it wants to "tell" something. Write a sentence to go with your picture. Use a word that begins with *gn, kn,* or *wr* in your sentence.

Antonyms

> **REMEMBER:** **Antonyms** are words that have opposite or nearly opposite meanings. *Stop* and *go* are antonyms. *Tall* and *short* are also antonyms.

A. Read each sentence. Write the word that is the opposite in meaning to the underlined word.

1. It is <u>fiction</u> that porcupines shoot their quills.

fact

sad

2. A porcupine's quills have <u>tiny</u> hooks.

large

hot

3. If an animal tries to <u>hurt</u> the porcupine, the quills stand on end.

help

stop

4. The porcupine turns around and backs up to his <u>enemy</u>.

friend

mother

B. On another paper, write a sentence about an animal. Use a pair of antonyms in your sentence.

NAME _____

Long Word Decoding

REMEMBER: When you try to read a long word, look for words and word parts you know.

A. Circle the words or word parts you know. Underline the vowel letters.

blizzard   desert   hospital   humble   pineapple

B. Write one of the words in Part A to answer each question.

1. Which word names a kind of fruit?

2. Which word means the opposite of *proud*?

3. Which word names a hot, sandy place?

4. Which word means ''a bad snowstorm''?

5. Which word names a building where sick people go?

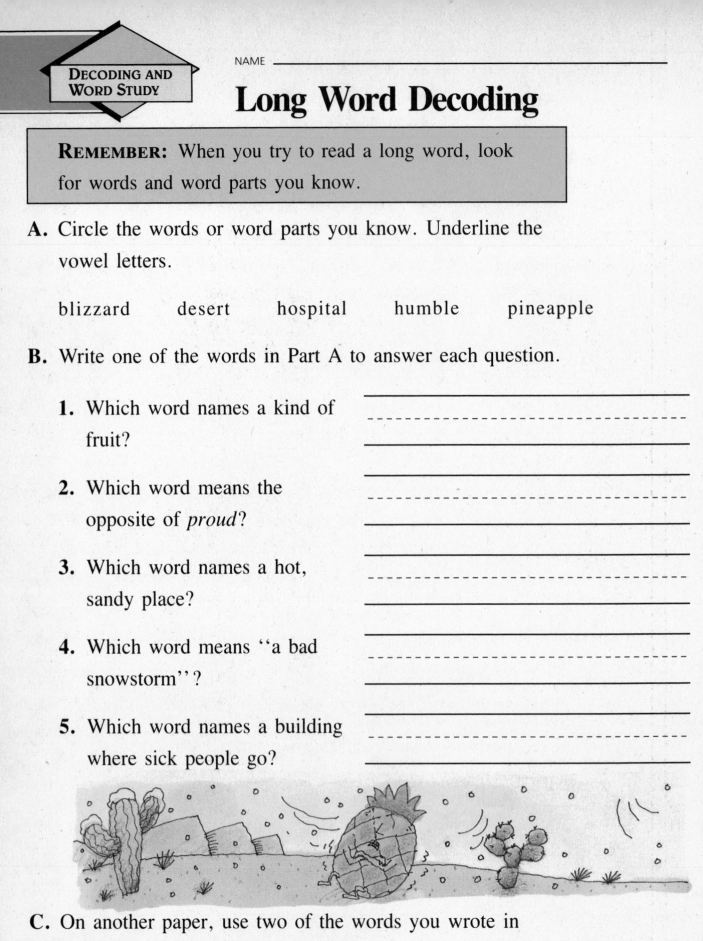

C. On another paper, use two of the words you wrote in Part B to write a sentence of your own.

Words with *oi, oy*

> **REMEMBER:** The letters *oi* and *oy* can stand for the
> vowel sound you hear in *oil* and *boy*.
> The b<u>oy</u> saw the bird put its head in the s<u>oi</u>l.

A. Read the stories. Then answer the questions. Each
answer should have the same sound as in *oil* and *boy*.

1. When ducks swim, they don't get wet. Their feathers are covered
with a special oil. The oil stops the water and keeps the ducks dry.

_____

- - - - - - - - - - - - - - - - - - -

What keeps ducks dry in water? _____

2. Some birds can say the things they hear. But they do not know
what the words mean. Our words are just a kind of interesting noise
to them.

_____

- - - - - - - - - - - - - - - - - - -

What do our words sound like to birds? _____

3. People have trained dogs to help them hunt. When the dog smells a
rabbit or a bird, it stops. The dog points at the animal with its
nose. That is why some dogs are called "pointers."

_____

- - - - - - - - - - - - - - - - - - -

What do some hunting dogs do with their noses? _____

B. On another paper, write two sentences that
tell something about an animal. Use as many
words with *oi* and *oy* as you can.

NAME _____

Using New Words

A. Write the words to finish the story.

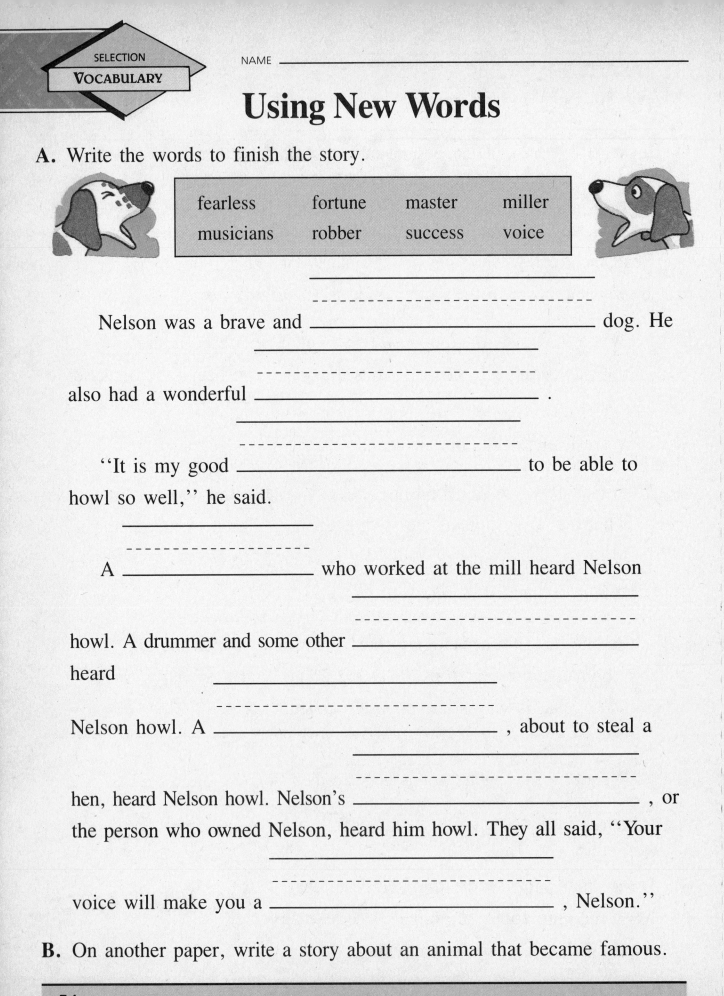

fearless	fortune	master	miller
musicians	robber	success	voice

Nelson was a brave and _____ dog. He

also had a wonderful _____ .

"It is my good _____ to be able to

howl so well," he said.

A _____ who worked at the mill heard Nelson

howl. A drummer and some other _____

heard

_____

Nelson howl. A _____ , about to steal a

hen, heard Nelson howl. Nelson's _____ , or

the person who owned Nelson, heard him howl. They all said, "Your

voice will make you a _____ , Nelson."

B. On another paper, write a story about an animal that became famous.

The Bremen Town Musicians

A. Write one or more words on each line to finish the story
about "The Bremen Town Musicians."

cat	house	kicked	ran away for good	robbers

_____

This story is about a donkey, a _____ , a rooster, and
a dog. They were musicians. Together they set out for Bremen.

The animals stopped in the woods at night to sleep. Following a

_____

light, they went up to a _____ . Inside, they

_____

saw food—and _____ !

The animals frightened the robbers away. That night the youngest
robber came back, but he did not stay long. The cat scratched him.

_____

The dog bit him. The donkey _____ him.
The rooster crowed at him.

_____

All of the robbers were so scared that they _____

_____ . The Bremen town

musicians stayed together in the house for the rest of their days.

B. Imagine you are the youngest robber. What would you
have told the other robbers after you ran from the house?
On another paper, write three sentences.

NAME _____

Words with *t*

> **REMEMBER:** The letter *t* can stand for the sound you
> hear in the middle of *fortune*.

A. Write the word that makes sense in each sentence and
has the letter *t* that stands for the sound in the middle of
fortune.

1. The animals loved their new house. They loved the beautiful

   _____

   -

   _____ .

   nature   furniture   store   _____

   -

2. The walls of the house were filled with _____ .

                               pictures   future   paintings

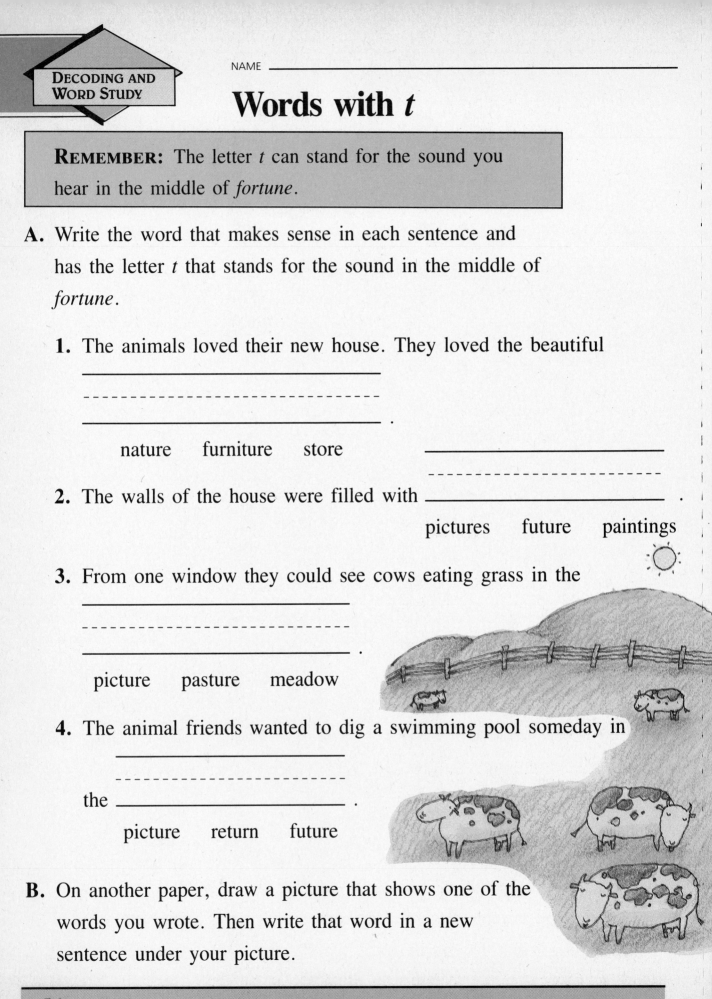

3. From one window they could see cows eating grass in the

   _____

   -

   _____ .

   picture   pasture   meadow

4. The animal friends wanted to dig a swimming pool someday in

   _____

   -

   the _____ .

   picture   return   future

B. On another paper, draw a picture that shows one of the
words you wrote. Then write that word in a new
sentence under your picture.

         Consonant *t* /ch/

Words with *oi, oy*

> **REMEMBER:** The letters *oi* and *oy* can stand for the vowel sound you hear in *oil* or *boy*.

A. Write the word that makes sense in each sentence.

enjoy   join   spoil   voice

1. Do you like music? What kind of music do

_____

----

you _____ most?

2. Maybe you would like to sing. Do you have a good

_____

----

singing _____ ?

3. Sometimes people get together to play music. Would

_____

----

you _____ with other people to make music?

4. Musicians need to play with great care. One careless note

_____

----

can _____ the song.

B. On another paper, write two sentences about making
music together. Use one of the words you wrote in
Part A.

NAME

Suffixes *-ful, -less*

> **REMEMBER:** The suffix *-ful* means "full of." The
> suffix *-less* means "without."

A. Read the sentences. Add *-ful* or *-less* to each underlined
word. Write the new word on the line.

1. The land was very cold. Snow was everywhere. Not a <u>cloud</u> was in

   _____

   the sky. The sky was _____ .

2. The wind was still. Nothing moved. The land was filled with <u>peace</u>.

   _____

   The land was very _____ .

3. On top of a hill was a small black tree. It had no leaves. No other

   kind of <u>life</u> seemed to be there. The land <u>seemed</u> to be

   _____

   _____ .

4. Suddenly a small red bird flew up to the tree. It landed on a dark

   branch. Then it sang. Its song filled the air with <u>hope</u>. It was

   _____

   a _____ song.

B. On another paper write two sentences that tell about the singing
bird. Use words with the suffixes *-ful* and *-less*.

Sequence

> **REMEMBER: Sequence** is the order in which things happen in a story. Look for signal words and story clues to figure out the sequence.

A. Write the sentences in the order they happened.

1. First the rooster saw a light in the dark woods. Then the donkey looked in through the window. Next the animals found the light was coming from a house.

1. _____

2. _____

3. _____

2. The animals stayed in the robbers' house. The robbers ran away from their house. The animals' song frightened the robbers.

1. _____

2. _____

3. _____

B. On another paper, write a sentence that tells what happened just after the donkey looked in the window.

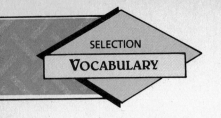
Using New Words

A. Read the story about making mittens. Write the word
that means the same thing as the underlined word or words.

combs	design	dye	loom	scissors	weave	wool	yarn

1. My best mittens are made
   from <u>the soft hairs of an
   animal</u>.

2. <u>Tools for cutting</u> were used to
   get the hair.

3. Then someone used <u>tools with
   hard teeth</u> to clean the hair.

4. The hairs were made into
   <u>strings of hairs put together</u>.

5. <u>Color</u> was added to make the
   yarn a beautiful red.

6. Next, someone had to <u>pass
   threads over and under</u> the
   cloth.

7. A <u>frame to stretch the hairs
   out on</u> was used to do this.

8. Grandma followed a <u>drawing</u>
   to make my mittens.

B. On another paper, write a sentences about a design you saw.

NAME _____

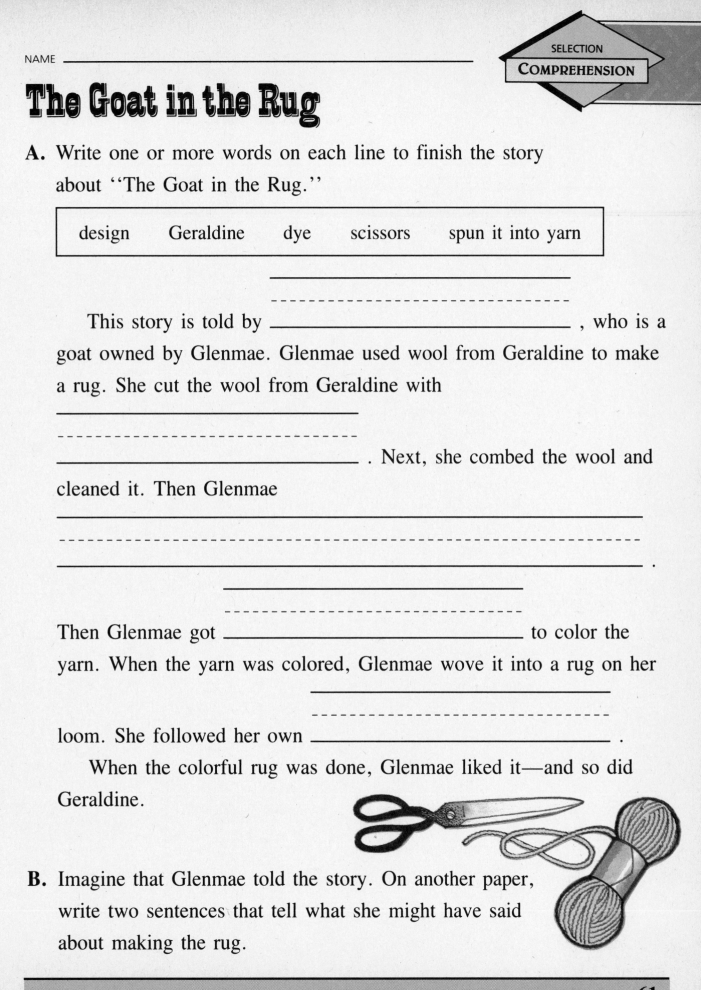

The Goat in the Rug

A. Write one or more words on each line to finish the story about ''The Goat in the Rug.''

design	Geraldine	dye	scissors	spun it into yarn

_____

- -

    This story is told by _____ , who is a goat owned by Glenmae. Glenmae used wool from Geraldine to make a rug. She cut the wool from Geraldine with

_____

- -

_____ . Next, she combed the wool and cleaned it. Then Glenmae

_____

- -

_____ .

_____

- -

Then Glenmae got _____ to color the yarn. When the yarn was colored, Glenmae wove it into a rug on her

_____

- -

loom. She followed her own _____ .

    When the colorful rug was done, Glenmae liked it—and so did Geraldine.

B. Imagine that Glenmae told the story. On another paper, write two sentences that tell what she might have said about making the rug.

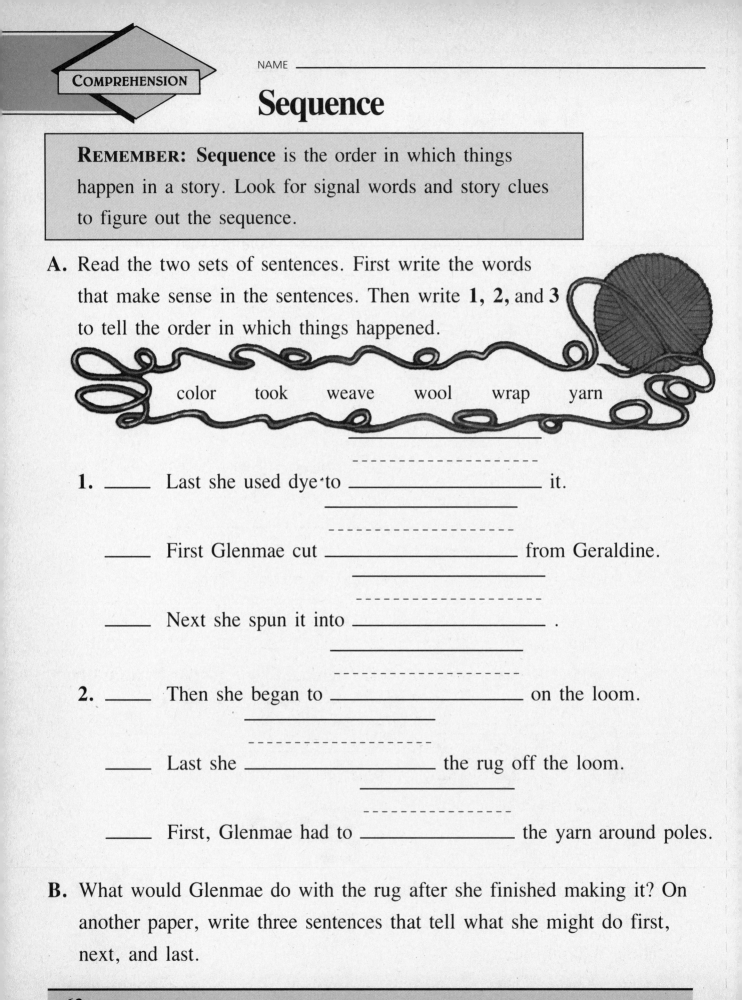

COMPREHENSION

Sequence

> **REMEMBER:** **Sequence** is the order in which things happen in a story. Look for signal words and story clues to figure out the sequence.

A. Read the two sets of sentences. First write the words that make sense in the sentences. Then write **1, 2,** and **3** to tell the order in which things happened.

color   took   weave   wool   wrap   yarn

1. ____ Last she used dye to _____ it.

____ First Glenmae cut _____ from Geraldine.

____ Next she spun it into _____ .

2. ____ Then she began to _____ on the loom.

____ Last she _____ the rug off the loom.

____ First, Glenmae had to _____ the yarn around poles.

B. What would Glenmae do with the rug after she finished making it? On another paper, write three sentences that tell what she might do first, next, and last.

___

Words with *oi*, *oy*

> **REMEMBER:** The letters *oi* and *oy* can stand for the
> vowel sound you hear in *oil* and *boy*.

A. Write the word that makes sense in each sentence. Each answer
should have the same vowel sound as in *oil* and *boy*.

_____

1. Geraldine did not _____ being clipped because it

                 like   enjoy   toy

   tickled.

2. Geraldine _____ Glenmae's dye plants by

             spoiled   wasted   boiled

   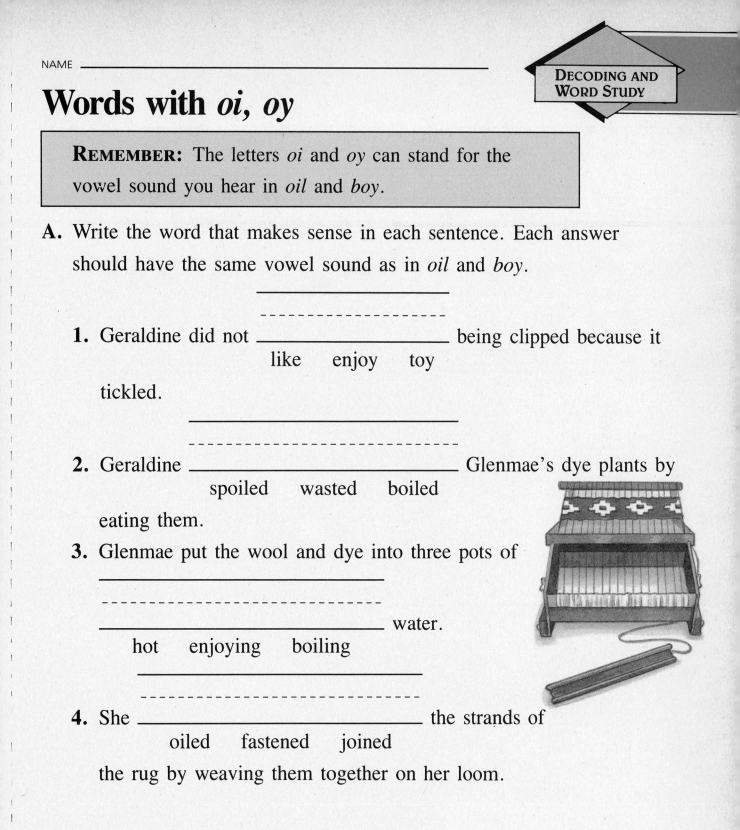

   eating them.

3. Glenmae put the wool and dye into three pots of

   _____

   _____ water.

      hot   enjoying   boiling

4. She _____ the strands of

         oiled   fastened   joined

   the rug by weaving them together on her loom.

B. Suppose you had helped Glenmae weave the rug, too.
On another paper, write a sentence about how you would
feel when the rug was finished.

Suffixes *-ful, -less*

> **REMEMBER:** The suffix *-ful* means "full of." The
> suffix *-less* means "without."

A. Write the word that makes sense in each sentence.

careful	colorful	cupful	spotless

1. Glenmae washed the wool. Not a spot was on it. Glenmae's wool

_____

was _____ .

2. She added one cup of dye to the pot. Glenmae added a

_____

_____ of dye.

3. Glenmae worked with great care at the loom. Her work was

_____

_____ .

4. The rug glowed with many colors. The rug was very

_____

_____ .

B. On another paper, write *careful* and *colorful*. Make new words
by changing the suffixes. Then write a new sentence using
each of the new words.

Drawing a Story Chain

REMEMBER: You can see how the main parts of a story fit together by drawing a story chain.

A. These words can help you finish the story chain for "The Goat in the Rug." Use them to tell about the steps Glenmae took to make the rug.

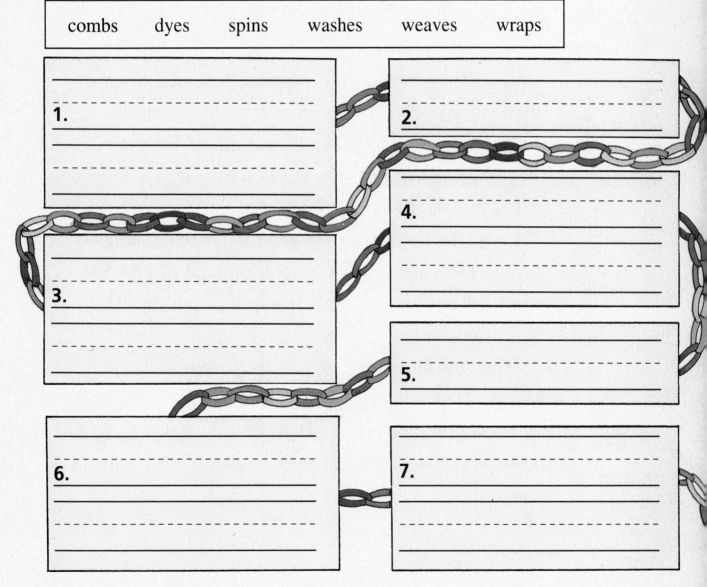

| combs | dyes | spins | washes | weaves | wraps |

1. _____

2. _____

3. _____

4. _____

5. _____

6. _____

7. _____

B. On another paper, make a story chain for your favorite story. Draw pictures to tell about the sentences you wrote in the story chain.

Checkpoint

Read the story. Then fill in the circle next to the correct answer.

Mammal mothers are the most loyal mothers of all. They stay with their babies longer than other animal mothers do. That is because mammal babies need a lot of care.

When baby kittens are born, for example, they are helpless. They cannot eat cat food. They need to have milk, and every mouthful comes from their mother. They cannot see at first, but they can hear her voice. They stay close to her. She is careful to clean them and keep them warm.

Later, the kittens can see and they become more playful. Then their mother becomes a kind of toy! She moves her tail for their endless chasing. But they still enjoy many peaceful times with their mother, too.

When the kittens get bigger, they seem to be fearless. They jump for joy and love to climb. They can eat a spoonful of cat food. They learn to clean themselves. But even then, their mother is watchful and near.

1. Which of these things can baby kittens do at <u>first</u>?
   - (a) They can clean themselves.
   - (b) They can jump and climb.
   - (c) They can drink milk.

2. Which of these things can baby kittens do <u>last</u>?
   - (a) They can eat cat food.
   - (b) They can see.
   - (c) They play with their mother's tail.

3. Which sentence tells you what kittens are like at <u>first</u>?
   - (a) They become more playful.
   - (b) When baby kittens are born, they are helpless.
   - (c) She is careful to clean them and keep them warm.

4. What does the mother cat do <u>first</u>?
   - (a) She moves her tail for the kittens to chase.
   - (b) She watches them run and climb.
   - (c) She keeps her kittens clean.

5. Which word has the same vowel sound as the underlined letters in *oil*?
   - (a) round
   - (b) only
   - (c) toy
   - (d) row

6. Which word meaning fits the underlined word in the sentence?
   The kittens look <u>peaceful</u>.
   - (a) no peace
   - (b) without peace
   - (c) full of peace

7. Which word has the same vowel sound as the underlined letters in *boy*?
   - (a) boat
   - (b) bowl
   - (c) bottle
   - (d) boil

8. Which word meaning fits the underlined word in the sentence?
   The bigger kittens are <u>fearless</u>.
   - (a) without fear
   - (b) having fear
   - (c) full of fear

NAME _____

Spelling Changes

> **REMEMBER:** When *y* comes after a consonant letter at the end of a word, you usually change the *y* to *i* before adding *-es* or *-ed*.

A. Read each sentence. Change the word under the line so that it makes sense in the sentence. Then write the word.

1. Glenmae loved to tell _____ as she

   story

   worked on her rugs.

2. She _____ to tell stories that would

   try

   make people happy.

3. She wanted to help people forget their _____ .

   worry

4. Glenmae's best story was about a mother dog and her four

   _____ .

   baby

5. The _____ loved to play

   puppy

   together.

B. On another paper, write a story about an animal. Use one of the words you wrote in Part A.

Using New Words

A. Write one word on each line to answer the questions.

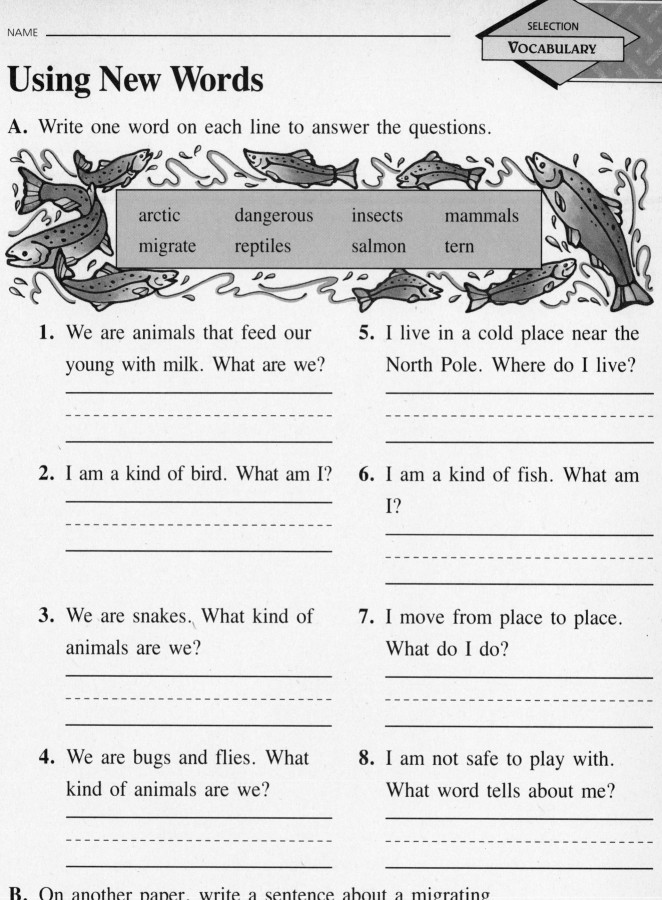

arctic   dangerous   insects   mammals

migrate   reptiles   salmon   tern

1. We are animals that feed our young with milk. What are we?

_____

- - - - - - - - - - - - - - - - - - -

_____

2. I am a kind of bird. What am I?

_____

- - - - - - - - - - - - - - - - - - -

_____

3. We are snakes. What kind of animals are we?

_____

- - - - - - - - - - - - - - - - - - -

_____

4. We are bugs and flies. What kind of animals are we?

_____

- - - - - - - - - - - - - - - - - - -

_____

5. I live in a cold place near the North Pole. Where do I live?

_____

- - - - - - - - - - - - - - - - - - -

_____

6. I am a kind of fish. What am I?

_____

- - - - - - - - - - - - - - - - - - -

_____

7. I move from place to place. What do I do?

_____

- - - - - - - - - - - - - - - - - - -

_____

8. I am not safe to play with. What word tells about me?

_____

- - - - - - - - - - - - - - - - - - -

_____

B. On another paper, write a sentence about a migrating animal.

Animals That Migrate

A. Write one or more words on each line to finish
the story about "Animals That Migrate."

arctic tern	Bering	California gray whale	migrate	need

_____

- -

    This story tells about animals that _____
They go long distances to get from one of their homes to the other.

    Animals migrate for different reasons. It may be because of the

_____

- -

weather. The _____ flies south in
winter to get away from the cold. The Chinook salmon returns to the
stream it came from to have babies. The

_____

- -

_____

migrates for food. It finds lots of krill and plankton in the

_____

- -

_____ Sea.

    Animals migrate because one home does not always have all they

_____

- -

_____ . Migration helps them to live.

B. Fold a paper in half. Draw two pictures of one of the animals
you read about. On one half, show the animal in its home.
On the other half, draw its home in the place it migrates to.
Write a sentence about each picture.

NAME _____

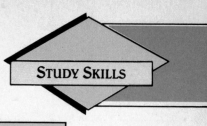
Maps

> **REMEMBER:** A **map** is a kind of picture of a place.
> Sometimes a map has a compass rose to help you find
> north, south, east, or west.

A. Use the map and its compass rose to help you finish
each sentence. Write **north, south, east,** or **west** on the
line.

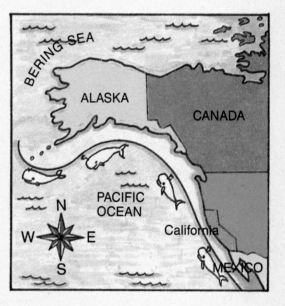

1. Gray whale babies are born in the
_____
- - - - - - - - - - - - - - - - - - - -
sea to the _____
of California and Mexico.

2. When the babies are big enough,
the whales travel along the Pacific
_____
- - - - - - - - - - - - - - - - - - - -
Coast to the _____ .

3. Finally the whales arrive at the Bering Sea. It is far to the
_____
- - - - - - - - - - - - - - - - - - - -
_____ of their winter home.

4. After a summer of eating in the arctic, the whales swim
_____
- - - - - - - - - - - - - - - - - - - -
_____ .

B. On another paper, draw a map that shows the migration of another
animal you have read about. Put a compass rose on your map to
show north, south, east, and west.

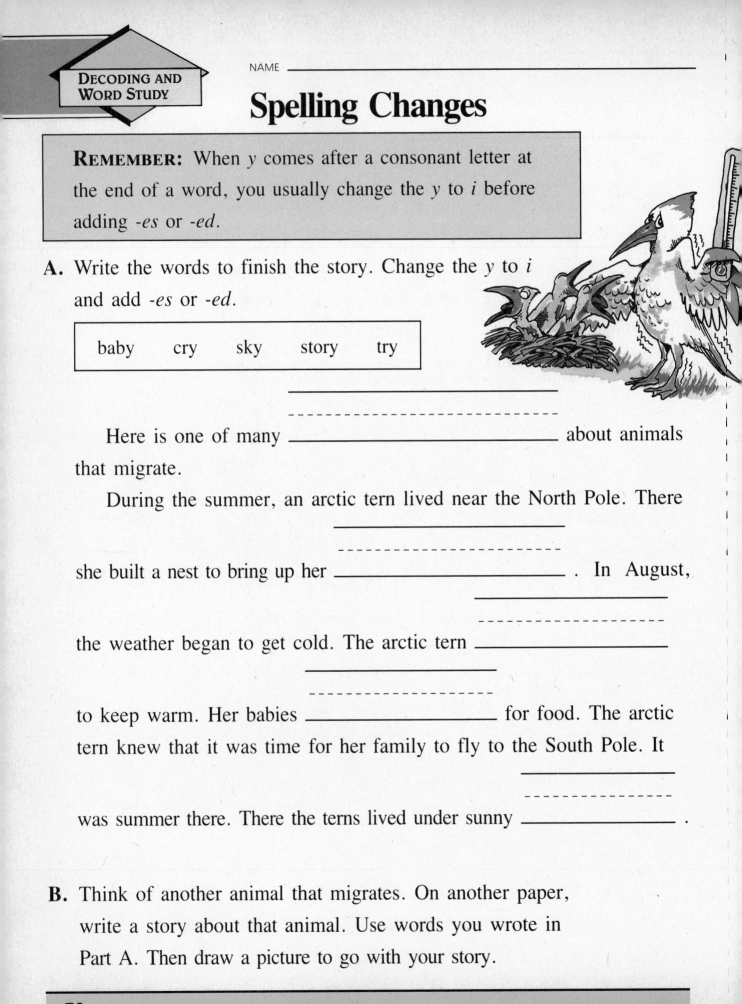

NAME _____

Spelling Changes

REMEMBER: When *y* comes after a consonant letter at the end of a word, you usually change the *y* to *i* before adding *-es* or *-ed*.

A. Write the words to finish the story. Change the *y* to *i* and add *-es* or *-ed*.

baby	cry	sky	story	try

_____

Here is one of many _____ about animals that migrate.

During the summer, an arctic tern lived near the North Pole. There _____

she built a nest to bring up her _____ . In August,

_____

the weather began to get cold. The arctic tern _____

_____

to keep warm. Her babies _____ for food. The arctic tern knew that it was time for her family to fly to the South Pole. It

_____

was summer there. There the terns lived under sunny _____ .

B. Think of another animal that migrates. On another paper, write a story about that animal. Use words you wrote in Part A. Then draw a picture to go with your story.

Antonyms

> **REMEMBER: Antonyms** are words that have opposite or nearly opposite meanings. *Stop* and *go* are antonyms.

A. Write the words that have opposite meanings.

cold	come	dangerous	few	go	hot	many	safe

1. You may think that only a _____ animals migrate.

In fact, _____ animals do.

2. A winter home may become too _____ . A summer

home may become too _____ .

3. Some animals need a _____ place for their babies. They

migrate to get away from _____ enemies.

4. Many animals _____ far away when they migrate. But

most of them _____ back!

B. On another paper, write two sentences about a trip. Use a pair of words that have opposite meanings.

NAME _____

Inference

> **REMEMBER:** Use story clues and what you already
> know to figure out things that the writer did not state.

A. Read each story. Then answer the questions about the
arctic tern and the salmon.

1. As the weather began to get cold at the North Pole, this animal got
   ready to fly to the South Pole. It was warmer there. What animal is

   this story about? _____

   _____

   How do you know? _____

   _____

   Why does this animal migrate? _____

2. After five years in the ocean, this animal returned to the stream it
   came from. This strong animal swam fast to make the dangerous
   trip. When it got back, the animal's babies were born.

   _____

   What animal is this story about? _____

   _____

   How do you know? _____

   _____

   Why does this animal migrate? _____

B. On another paper, write three sentences about an animal.
Give clues so that others can guess what it is.

Using New Words

A. Write one word on each line to finish the story.

cart	fellow	hobby	introduce
invited	pleasant	recognize	timid

_____

I was _____ to a hayride birthday party. I

only knew one _____ who was going to be there.

I felt _____ about going. I wondered who would

_____ me to the new people. Would I

_____ anyone at all?

_____

I went to the birthday party. I talked about my _____ .

All the boys and girls were _____ to me. At the

party, we all rode together in a _____ pulled by a horse.

B. On another paper, write three sentences about a time you met some
new people. Tell how you felt before you met them and how you felt
after you met them. Use as many story words as you can.

TOAD of TOAD HALL

A. Write one or more words on each line to finish the story about "Toad of Toad Hall."

Mole	motorcar	river	timid	Toad Hall

This story is about Rat, Toad, and Rat's new friend, Mole. Rat

_____   _____

liked to stay near the _____ , and _____

wanted to stay with Rat. They liked things to stay the same. Toad had

_____

another idea. He was not so _____ as Rat

and Mole. Toad liked new things to do. He wanted Rat and Mole to

_____

come to _____ . Then Alfred the Horse

came along, and Toad, Rat, and Mole all went for a ride in Toad's

cart. The next thing they knew, the cart was broken by a speeding

_____

_____ . Toad, always looking for

something new, thought that a motorcar was the only way to travel.

B. On another paper, draw pictures of Rat, Mole, and
Toad. Try to show what each one is like in your
pictures. Then write a sentence that tells why you want
Rat, Mole, or Toad to be your friend.

Multiple Meanings

> **REMEMBER:** Many words have more than one meaning.
> Use other words in the sentence to help you figure out
> which meaning is being used.

A. Use each word in two different sentences.

| bank   cart   law |

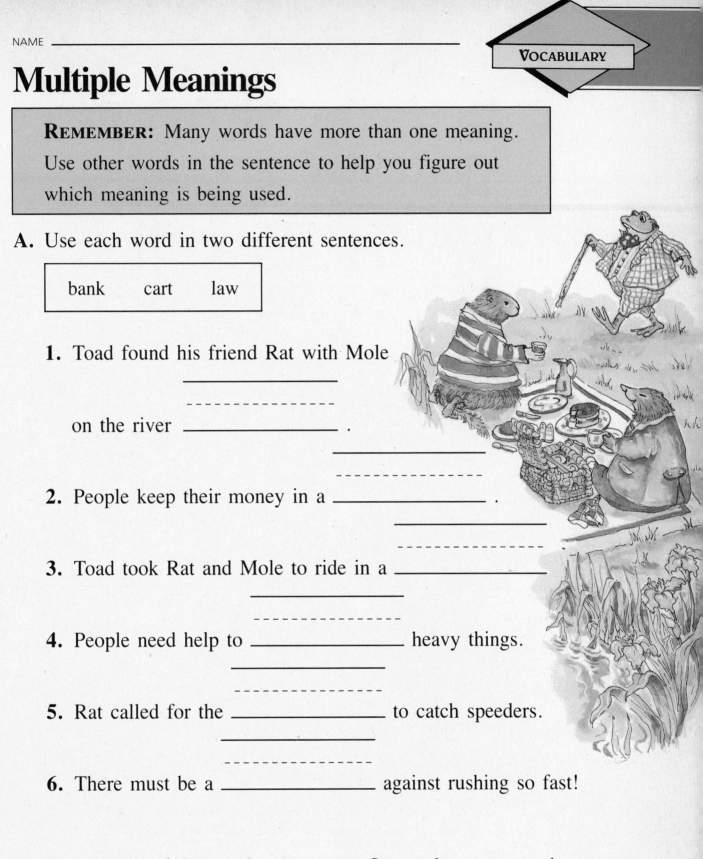

1. Toad found his friend Rat with Mole
   _____
   - - - - - - - - - - - - - - - -
   on the river _____ .
   _____
   - - - - - - - - - - - - - - - -

2. People keep their money in a _____ .
   _____
   - - - - - - - - - - - - - - - -

3. Toad took Rat and Mole to ride in a _____
   _____
   - - - - - - - - - - - - - - - -

4. People need help to _____ heavy things.
   _____
   - - - - - - - - - - - - - - - -

5. Rat called for the _____ to catch speeders.
   _____
   - - - - - - - - - - - - - - - -

6. There must be a _____ against rushing so fast!

B. Choose one of the words you wrote. On another paper, write two
sentences using the same word. Make each sentence show
a different meaning of the word.

NAME _____

Spelling Changes

REMEMBER: When *y* comes after a consonant letter at the end of a word, you usually change the *y* to *i* before adding *-es* or *-ed*.

A. Read the story. Write all the words in which the *y* has been changed to *i* before *-es* or *-ed* was added.

Toad has some unusual hobbies. He likes to tell stories about them. He told Rat about a time he tried to fly. He made wings from some dried leaves. He carried the wings all the way to the top of a tree. Birds and their babies were surprised when they saw him there. The bees and flies were surprised, too! Toad jumped from the tree and started to fly. He fell down with a bang. Poor Toad! It hurt so much he cried.

_____   _____

_____   _____

_____   _____

_____   _____

B. Think of another hobby for Toad. On another paper, write two sentences about the hobby.

Sequence

REMEMBER: Sequence is the order in which things happen in a story. Look for signal words and story clues to figure out the sequence.

A. Number the sentences in the right order to tell a story. Then write the sentences on the lines.

_____ The cart was broken and Toad was dazed.

_____ Rat and Mole got into the cart with Toad.

_____ Rat and Mole took care of Toad, helping him to walk.

_____ Toad wanted his friends to ride with him in the cart.

_____ A motorcar came down the road at fifty miles an hour.

_____
_____
_____
_____
_____
_____
_____
_____

B. Fold another paper into three parts. Draw pictures to go with three of the sentences from Part A. Draw them in the order they happened in the story.

Checkpoint

Read the story. Then fill in the circle next to the correct answer.

A bat is a strange and wonderful animal. It flies and hunts at night. It hangs upside down and sleeps during the day. Many people think things about bats that are not true. Some people think that bats are birds. Others have the idea that they are blind. Some people are afraid that bats will fly into their hair. But these things are not true.

The <u>fact</u> is that bats are mammals. <u>Mother</u> bats feed their babies milk from their bodies, just like all mammal mothers do. All bats can see, but they do not use their eyes to find things. They have a special way of using their ears to know where things are, even in the <u>dark</u>. That is why a bat will not fly into your hair.

People believe many strange stories about bats. But most of the stories are fiction. The next time you see the night skies filled with flying bats, you will know the facts!

1. Which word fits into this sentence from the story? The bat ___ and hunts at night.
   - (a) fly
   - (b) flies
   - (c) flew

2. Which word is the opposite of the underlined word *fact*?
   - (a) true
   - (b) story
   - (c) fiction

3. Which sentence from the story helps you know the opposite of *fact*?
   - (a) A bat is a strange and wonderful animal.
   - (b) Others have the idea that they are blind.
   - (c) But these things are not true.

4. Which word fits into this sentence from the story? Mother bats feed their ___ milk.
   - (a) babies
   - (b) baby
   - (c) babys

5. Which word is the opposite of the underlined word *mother*?
   - (a) sister
   - (b) brother
   - (c) father

6. Which word fits into this sentence from the story? People believe many strange ___ about bats.
   - (a) stories
   - (b) storys
   - (c) story

7. Which word is the opposite of the underlined word *dark*?
   - (a) night
   - (b) skies
   - (c) light

8. Which sentence from the story has the opposite of the word *night* in it?
   - (a) The fact is that bats are mammals.
   - (b) It hangs upside down and sleeps during the day.
   - (c) But these things are not true.

Vocabulary Review

Fill in the circle next to the word that best fits in the sentence.

1. It is a ___ that the earth moves around the sun.
   (a) fiction   (b) yarn   (c) fact   (d) tern

2. It is ___ to skate on thin ice.
   (a) tiny   (b) pleasant   (c) dangerous   (d) arctic

3. The ___ took the jewels from the store.
   (a) dye   (b) combs   (c) loom   (d) robber

4. Two horses pulled the big ___ loaded with hay.
   (a) cart   (b) fact   (c) fortune   (d) scissors

5. Judy used ___ to color her shirt.
   (a) wool   (b) miller   (c) fellow   (d) dye

6. Mike's ___ does not want him on the team.
   (a) design   (b) cart   (c) enemy   (d) wool

7. The story about Cinderella is ___ , because it could not really happen.
   (a) fact   (b) fiction   (c) robber   (d) timid

8. Dave is a very smart ___ in my math class.

   (a) cart   (b) wool   (c) fellow   (d) hobby

9. My brother's ___ is to collect stamps.

   (a) hobby   (b) enemy   (c) fellow   (d) master

10. Some kinds of ___ are dogs, bats, and cows.

   (a) musicians   (b) salmon   (c) mammals   (d) insects

11. The dog listened to his ___ and did what he was told.

   (a) cart   (b) master   (c) yarn   (d) fiction

12. The ___ played a lovely song.

   (a) mammals   (b) success   (c) reptiles   (d) musicians

13. Frank can ___ yarn into cloth.

   (a) shoot   (b) weave   (c) migrate   (d) recognize

14. A coat made of ___ is warm.

   (a) master   (b) cart   (c) hobby   (d) wool

15. Mother used ___ to weave that rug.

   (a) fact   (b) yarn   (c) mammals   (d) voice

NAME _____

Unit Wrap-Up

Write the answer to each question.

1. All the stories in this unit were about one kind of thing. What was that?

_____

- -

_____

_____

- -

_____

2. In what way were the stories "Animal Fact and Fiction" and "Animals That Migrate" alike?

_____

- -

_____

_____

- -

_____

3. Were the animals in the stories "The Bremen Town Musicians" and "Toad of Toad Hall" real or not real? How could you tell?

_____

- -

_____

_____

- -

_____

What Interests Me

Circle the pictures that show things you like to read about.
Use the chart to find out which books you would enjoy.

1	2	3	4	BOOK LIST
★			★	*The Great Town and Country Bicycle Balloon Chase* by Barbara Douglass
★	★	★		*Summer Business* by Charles E. Martin
		★	★	*The Little Engine That Could* by Watty Piper
		★	★	*Katy and the Big Snow* by Virginia Lee Burton
★	★			*Mr. Plum's Paradise* by Elsa Trimby

NAME _____

My Book List

Name of Book

_____
- -
_____

Author

_____
- -
_____

Name of Book

_____
- -
_____

Author

_____
- -
_____

Drawing Conclusions

> **REMEMBER:** When you **draw a conclusion,** you figure out things that are not explained in a story. Use story clues and what you already know to draw a conclusion.

A. Read each paragraph. Then write the answers to the questions.

1. The shoemaker got out of bed. He crept down the stairs. It was dark, but he could see the elves. They were making beautiful shoes.

_____

- -

What time of day was it? _____

2. The shoemaker said, ''The elves have made beautiful shoes. We are not poor any longer. Isn't that wonderful, my love?''

_____

- -

To whom was the shoemaker talking? _____

3. A man came into the shoemaker's shop. He said, ''I need some boots. They must keep my feet warm and dry. And they must keep out the snow.''

_____

- -

What time of the year was it? _____

B. How do you think the shoemaker felt when he saw the shoes the elves made? On another paper, write your answer.

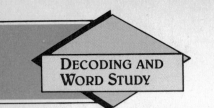

NAME _____

Words with *ou, ow (soul, flow)*

> **REMEMBER:** The letters *ou* and *ow* can stand for the
> vowel sound you hear in *soul* and *flow*.

A. Read each sentence. Circle the word in which you hear the same
vowel sound as in *soul* and *flow*. Then write the word.

1. I'll throw a baseball hard.

    _____

2. I'll make bread out of dough.

    _____

3. I'll row across the lake.

    _____

4. I'll know everything at school.

    _____

5. When I grow up, I'll be great!

    _____

B. On another paper, write a sentence that tells one thing
you would like to do when you grow up.

Using New Words

A. Write the words to finish the story.

frames	slid	snowman	wipers
office	snowflake	windshield	

_____

Dad had to go to his _____

to work. But snow was falling. Snow fell on his face and hair.

_____

It fell on the _____ of his glasses. A

_____

_____ even got in his eye!

The glass _____ of the car was

_____

covered with snow. Dad turned on the _____

to push the snow away.

Then he started to drive away. But the road was covered with ice.

_____

The car _____ all over the street. Dad got out of the

car. ''This is no day for the office,'' he said. ''It's a day to make

_____

a _____ .'' And that is just what we did!

B. On another paper, write a sentence about the snowman
Dad helped to make.

WATCH OUT, RONALD MORGAN!

A. Write one word on each line to finish the story about
"Watch Out, Ronald Morgan!"

glasses   Ronald   school   snowman   unhappy

This story is about _____ , who wanted to
be a super kid. But he had trouble when he did things at

_____ . In kickball the ball bounced off his
head. He also had trouble cutting out a drawing he made of a snowflake.

Ronald got a pair of _____ . He was sure
he would be super after that. But he still had trouble doing things

right. He was so _____ he took off his
new glasses. His teacher asked Ronald to try wearing his glasses again.
The next day, he put on his glasses again and drew a super

_____ . Ronald had gotten used to his new
glasses.

B. On another paper, draw a picture of the part of the story you liked
best. Write a sentence about your picture.

Other Vowel Sounds

> **REMEMBER:** The letter *o* can stand for the vowel sound you hear in *love* or *moth*.

A. Read each sentence and the words under it. Write on the line the word that makes sense in the sentence. Each word should have the vowel sound you hear in *love* or *moth*.

1. Cold _____ was in the air when Ronald left school.

    snow   frost   hot

2. Ronald looked at the sky _____ .

    over   love   above

3. "I left my _____ at home," said Ronald.

    gloves   coat   doves

4. Ronald _____ his hands deep into his pockets.

    pushed   shoved   tossed

5. Ronald's hands stayed warm during the _____ walk.

    long   short   song

B. Take word parts you know from the end of two of the answers you wrote in Part A. You will have two words that rhyme with another word you wrote. Write the three rhyming words on another paper.

NAME _____

Words with *ou, ow (soul, flow)*

REMEMBER: The letters *ou* and *ow* can stand for the vowel sound you hear in *soul* and *flow*.

A. Read each set of words. Circle the word that has the vowel sound you hear in *soul* and *flow*.

1. about	now	low
2. slow	plow	you
3. bounce	wow	though
4. howl	throw	shout

B. Use the words you circled in Part A to finish the sentences.

_____
- -

1. _____ Ronald had new glasses, he was not a super kid.

_____
- -

2. He couldn't _____ a ball any harder.

_____
- -

3. He was still a _____ runner.

4. But Ronald's new glasses helped him see everything, high

_____
- -

and _____ .

C. On another paper, write two sentences about what Ronald could do when he got used to his glasses.

Multiple Meanings

> **REMEMBER:** Many words have more than one meaning. Use other words in the sentence to help you figure out which meaning is being used.

A. Write the letter of the correct meaning of each underlined word.

1. rock **a.** go back and forth **b.** a stone   _____

I like to <u>rock</u> in this chair.   _____

Peter found a <u>rock</u> that was green.   _____

2. bit **a.** a little part **b.** took a bite   _____

She <u>bit</u> into the fruit and said, "Good!"   _____

Then she gave a <u>bit</u> of it to the dog.   _____

3. fall **a.** go down **b.** time of the year   _____

He saw the box <u>fall</u>, and he caught it.   _____

Each <u>fall</u> we go back to school.   _____

4. train **a.** way to travel **b.** teach   _____

Jan will <u>train</u> her puppy to sit up.   _____

We went to the city by <u>train</u>.   _____

B. On another paper, write two sentences, each showing a different meaning for the word *pitcher*.

"Watch Out, Ronald Morgan!" **93**

Words with *au, aw*

> **REMEMBER:** The letters *au* and *aw* can stand for the vowel sound you hear in *pause* and *jaw*.

A. Write the word that makes sense in each sentence. Each word should have the same vowel sound as in *pause* and *jaw*.

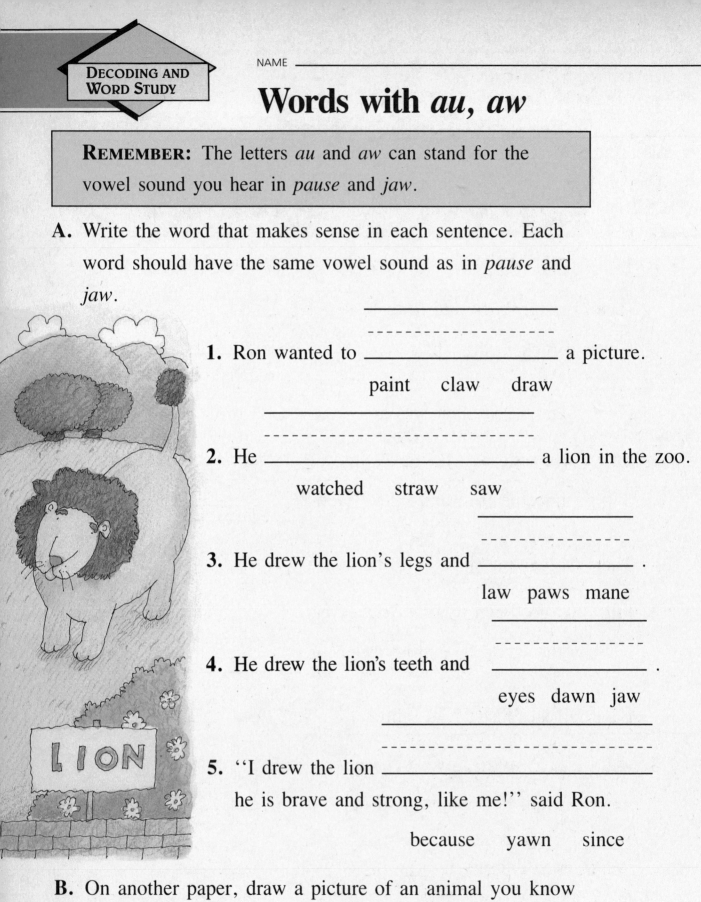

1. Ron wanted to _____ a picture.

     paint   claw   draw

2. He _____ a lion in the zoo.

   watched   straw   saw

3. He drew the lion's legs and _____ .

    law   paws   mane

4. He drew the lion's teeth and _____ .

     eyes   dawn   jaw

5. "I drew the lion _____ he is brave and strong, like me!" said Ron.

          because   yawn   since

B. On another paper, draw a picture of an animal you know well. Then write two sentences that tell what the animal looks like. Use at least one word with *au* or *aw*.

DANDELION

A. Write the words that might tell about the hat in the picture.
The first letter of each word is given.

| address | dapper | elegant | magnificent |
| poured | promise | stylish | unruly |

m _____   e _____

s _____   d _____

B. Write the words that can take the place of the underlined words.

1. Susie said to Tim, "Give me
   your word that you'll come to
   my house."
   _____
   "I'll be there," said Tim.
   _____

2. But he forgot Susie's street
   and house number.
   _____

3. Then the rain flowed down
   on him.
   _____

4. All that water made Tim's
   shirt messy. Tim was glad
   when he got to the house.
   _____

C. On another paper, write a sentence about the hat.

DANDELION

A. Write one or more words on each line to finish the story about "Dandelion."

| bouquet of flowers | Dandelion | himself | in the rain | know |

_____

This story is about _____ , who got invited to Jennifer Giraffe's party. Dandelion wanted to be very dapper for the party. So he curled his hair. He bought new clothes. He got

_____

Jennifer a _____ .

When Dandelion got to the party, Jennifer Giraffe did not

_____

even _____ who he was! She did not let Dandelion in. _____

Then Dandelion got caught _____ .
His clothes got wet. His hair lost its curl. When he was dry, he rang the bell again. This time, Jennifer knew him.

Dandelion promised that he would never try to be a dandy again.

_____

He would always be _____ !

B. Imagine that you are Dandelion. On another paper, write to a friend about what happened to you at the party. Also write about what you are going to do the next time you go to a party.

NAME _____

Words with *gn, kn, wr*

REMEMBER: The letters *gn, kn,* and *wr* can stand for the sound you hear at the beginning of *gnaw, know,* and *write*.

A. Use the words in the box to finish the poem.

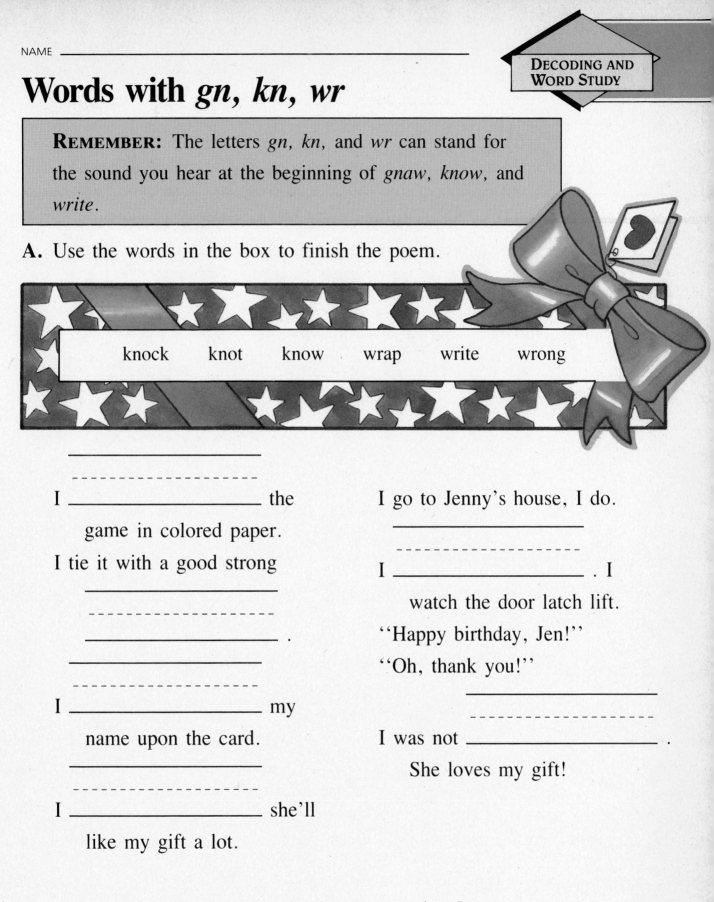

knock   knot   know   wrap   write   wrong

_____

I _____ the
  game in colored paper.
I tie it with a good strong
  _____
  _____ .
  _____
I _____ my
  name upon the card.
  _____
I _____ she'll
  like my gift a lot.

I go to Jenny's house, I do.
  _____
I _____ . I
  watch the door latch lift.
"Happy birthday, Jen!"
"Oh, thank you!"
  _____
I was not _____ .
  She loves my gift!

B. On another paper, write a thank-you note that Jenny might write to Dandelion.

NAME _____

Words with *au*, *aw*

> **REMEMBER:** The letters *au* and *aw* can stand for the vowel sound you hear in *pause* and *jaw*.

A. Write the words to finish the poem. Each word should have the same vowel sound as in *pause* and *jaw*.

Proud Cat

lawn
grass
draw

_____
- - - - - - - - - - - - - - - - - - -
Dapper, I walk upon the _____ .

fawn
dawn
light

_____
- - - - - - - - - - - - - - - - - - -
It's early morning. It is _____ .

run
law
pause

_____
- - - - - - - - - - - - - - - - - - -
I look around. I turn. I _____ .

yawn
straw
stretch

_____
- - - - - - - - - - - - - - - - - - -
I close my eyes. I make an elegant _____ .

saw
claws
nails

_____
- - - - - - - - - - - - - - - - - - -
I show my stylish _____ .

Oh, why am I so magnificent?

why
because
jaw

_____
- -
Because, just _____ .

B. On another paper, draw a picture to go with this poem. Write a sentence that tells what the cat looks like. Use at least one word with *au* or *aw*.

Vowel Digraphs *au*, *aw* /ô/

Words with *ou, ow (soul, flow)*

> **REMEMBER:** The letters *ou* and *ow* can stand for the vowel sound you hear in *soul* and *flow*.

A. Write the word that makes sense in each sentence and has the vowel sound you hear in *soul* and *flow*.

1. Now the _____ is about to fall.

    rain   snow   flow

2. It comes down softly and _____ .

    slowly   gently   row

3. It _____ deeper, covering the ground.

    knows   gets   grows

4. Dandelion makes three big _____ .

    balls   snowballs   crows

5. A smiling _____ is standing near him.

    snowman   mailman   throw

B. On another paper, write a new sentence about Dandelion and the snow. Use a word with *ow* or *ou* as in *flow* and *soul* in the sentence.

Making a Character Chart

REMEMBER: You can learn more about the characters in a story by making a character chart. Think about something a character did or said. Then decide what it tells about the character.

A. Draw a line to match the thing Dandelion did or said with what it tells about him.

Things Dandelion Did

What It Tells About Him

1. Had his mane curled for the party

A. Was a thoughtful guest

2. Tried again to go to the party

B. Could laugh at the silly things he did

3. Brought flowers to Jennifer Giraffe

C. Wanted to look great for Jennifer's party

4. Laughed and roared, "I was that silly-looking lion!"

D. Did not easily give up on something he wanted to do

B. Read the sentence and decide what it tells you about Dandelion.

But now Dandelion thought he really should wear something more elegant than a sweater to the party.

Write what you think about Dandelion on another paper. Begin your sentence like this:

I think that Dandelion ___ .

Words with *ew*

> **REMEMBER:** The letters *ew* can stand for the vowel
> sounds you hear in *flew* and *few*.

A. Read each set of words. Circle the word that has the
vowel sound you hear in either *flew* or *few*.

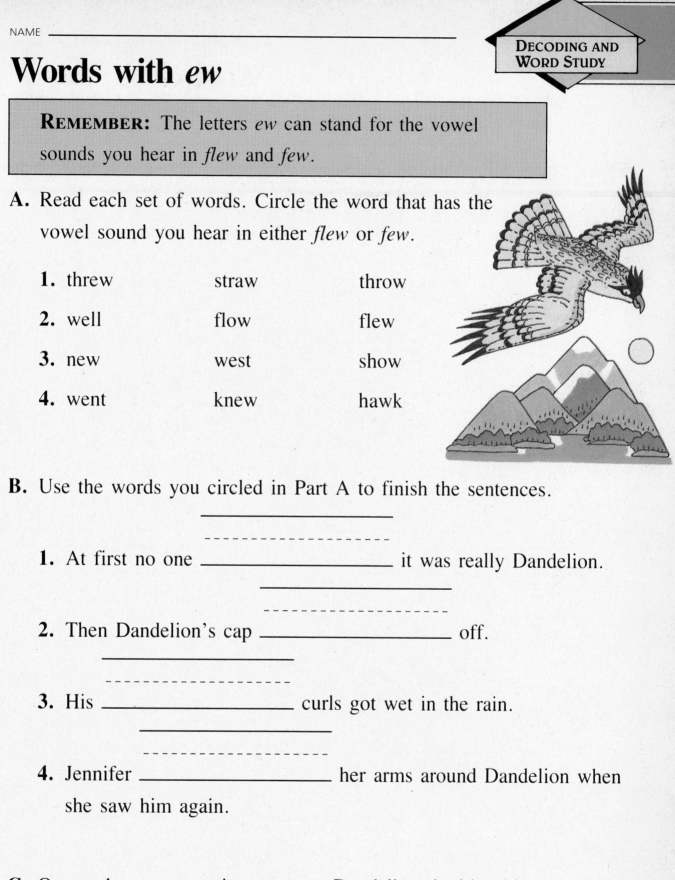

1. threw	straw	throw
2. well	flow	flew
3. new	west	show
4. went	knew	hawk

B. Use the words you circled in Part A to finish the sentences.

1. At first no one _____ it was really Dandelion.

2. Then Dandelion's cap _____ off.

3. His _____ curls got wet in the rain.

4. Jennifer _____ her arms around Dandelion when
she saw him again.

C. On another paper, write a note to Dandelion, inviting him to a party
you want to have.

NAME _____

Using New Words

A. Write one word on each line to finish the sentence.

| challenge | goal | nickname | score |
| cousin | goalie | rules | sports |

1. David likes to play many _____ .

2. He liked to _____ others to play soccer.

3. David knew all the _____ of the game.

4. Rosie's _____ , William, also played soccer.

5. William's _____ was "Silly Billy," because he always told silly jokes.

6. One day Rosie played _____ .

7. Silly Billy kicked the ball across the _____ .

8. The _____ was 2–1.

B. On another paper, write two sentences about a game you play with others.

S⚽CCER SAM

A. Write one or more words on each line to finish the story about "Soccer Sam."

Marco	Mexico	six goals	soccer	use his hands

This story is about Sam and his cousin who visited him.

_____

The cousin's name was _____ .

_____

He came from _____ to visit Sam and Sam's family in the United States.

When Marco played basketball the first time, the boys laughed at him. Marco did not know how to play the game. He did

_____

not _____ . Then Marco showed the boys how to play a game he knew. It was called

_____

_____ . The boys liked the game a lot. They asked Marco to help them practice.

The second graders challenged the third graders to a soccer game. The best players in the game were Sam and Marco. They each

_____

scored _____ . The second graders won!

B. On another paper, write three sentences telling how you think Marco felt when his class won.

NAME _____

Words with *gh*

> **REMEMBER:** The letters *gh* can stand for the sound you hear at the end of *laugh*.

A. Write the words to finish the poem about Marco and Sam. Each word should have the sound you hear at the end of *laugh*.

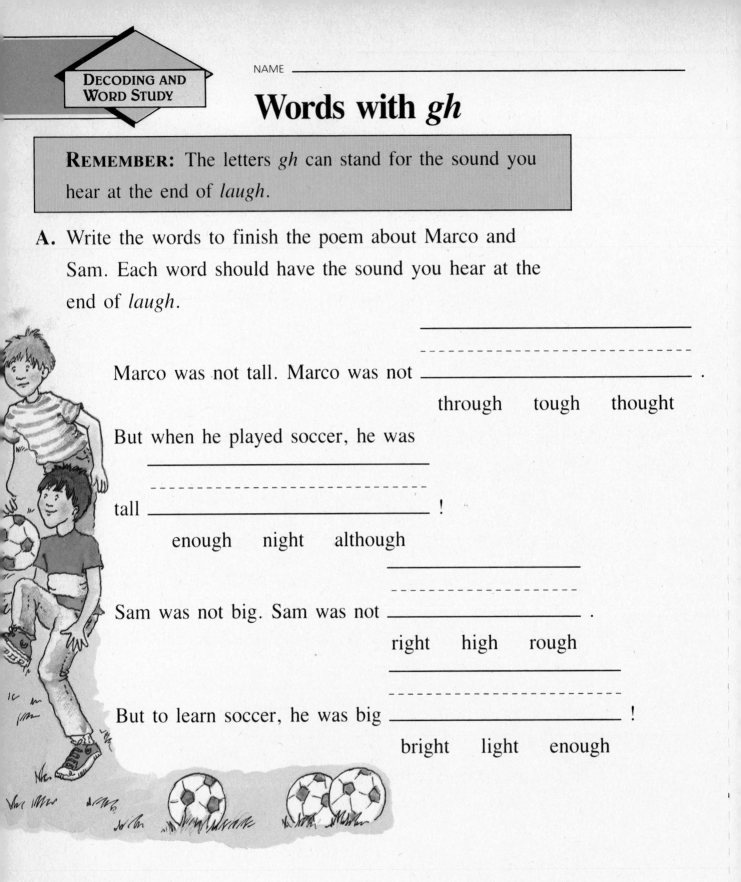

Marco was not tall. Marco was not _____ .

through   tough   thought

But when he played soccer, he was

_____

tall _____ !

enough   night   although

_____

Sam was not big. Sam was not _____ .

right   high   rough

_____

But to learn soccer, he was big _____ !

bright   light   enough

B. On another paper, draw a picture that shows Marco scoring a goal. Write a sentence to go with your picture. Use one word with *gh* in your sentence.

Words with *s'*

REMEMBER: To show that more than one person owns something, add *s'*.

A. Write the word that belongs in the sentence.

1. The children will play soccer with the second

   _____

   -

   _____ ball.

   graders'   grader's   graders

2. The second graders will try to get the ball in the third

   _____

   -

   _____ goal.

   graders'   grader's   graders

3. The _____ job is to stop the ball.

   goalies'   goalie's   goalies

   _____

   -

4. Both _____ goalies have played well

   before.

   teams   teams'   team's

B. On another paper, write two sentences about learning how to play a new sport or game. Use at least one word with *s'* in your sentence.

NAME _____

Words with *ew*

REMEMBER: The letters *ew* can stand for the vowel sounds you hear in *flew* and *few*.

A. Write the word that makes sense in each sentence and has the vowel sound you hear in either *flew* or *few*.

_____

- -

1. Marco _____ how to play soccer.

learned   grew   knew

_____

- - - - - - - - - - - - - -

2. Marco made _____ friends.

drew   many   new

_____

- - - - - - - - - - - - - - - - - - - -

3. Marco and his friend Rick had _____ for dinner at Rick's house.   steak   few   stew

_____

- -

4. Marco _____ two inches that year.

knew   became   grew

_____

- - - - - - - - - - - - - -

5. Marco _____ home on a big jet.

flew   few   went

B. Imagine you are Marco. How would you tell your friends in Mexico about basketball? On another paper, write two sentences about basketball or another game. Use two words with *ew*.

Long Word Decoding

> **REMEMBER:** When you try to read a long word, look
> for words and word parts you know.

A. Circle the words or word parts you know. Underline the
vowel letters.

basket   pickle   outside   motel   watchful

B. Write one of the words in Part A to answer each question.

1. Which word means "a place to
   stay overnight"?

2. Which word means "a cucumber
   kept in vinegar"?

3. Which word means the
   opposite of *inside*?

4. Which word means the same
   as *alert*?

5. Which word names a kind
   of container?

C. On another paper, use two of the words you wrote in
Part B to write a sentence of your own.

Checkpoint

Read the story. Then fill in the circle next to the correct answer.

They call me the Hawk. I find what can't be found and catch what can't be caught. I've taught the kids on my street to bring their problems to me.

On Friday, they told me the old yellow house was haunted. They heard sounds and saw tracks in the snow. I had to yawn. I'm not afraid of anything. "I'll go in at dawn," I said.

Early on Saturday, every kid on the street showed up. "I'm going in to find the cause of what you heard and saw," I said. I went to a window. I had to pause. I couldn't go in. I was afraid. I thought fast, though. "I'll need help," I said. We flipped coins. Three kids came in with me. We found a sparrow family. We left them alone.

They call me the Hawk. And these are my friends, Shadow, Crow, and Jaws. We work together. The kids on our street bring their problems to us.

1. Which word has the same vowel sound as the underlined letters in *paw*?

  ⓐ how

  ⓑ haunted

  ⓒ hope

  ⓓ hand

4. Which word has the same vowel sound as the underlined letters in *jaw*?

  ⓐ throw

  ⓑ though

  ⓒ through

  ⓓ taught

2. Which word has the same vowel sound as the underlined letters in *flow*?

  ⓐ touch

  ⓑ town

  ⓒ though

  ⓓ taught

5. Which word has the same vowel sound as the underlined letters in *soul*?

  ⓐ saw

  ⓑ sparrow

  ⓒ straw

  ⓓ spun

3. Which word has the same vowel sound as the underlined letters in *cause*?

  ⓐ you

  ⓑ yellow

  ⓒ yard

  ⓓ yawn

6. Which word has the same vowel sound as the underlined letters in *paw*?

  ⓐ could

  ⓑ coat

  ⓒ cow

  ⓓ caught

NAME _____

Predicting Outcomes

REMEMBER: When you **predict,** you make a guess about what will happen in a story. Use story clues and what you know to make a good prediction.

A. Read the story. Guess what will happen next. Write your guess on the line.

1. Marco showed the second graders how to play soccer. He taught them how to pass and kick. They were fast learners. The second graders practiced all week. Soon it would be the big day.

_____

The second graders will _____.

play a game   quit the team

2. The third graders lost the game. In third grade, there was nobody like Marco who could show them how to play the game. They challenged the second graders to another game.
The second graders

_____

_____

will not play again   will play again

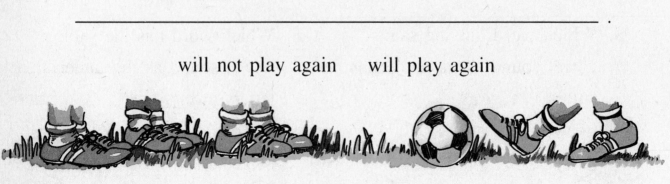

B. Do you think soccer will become a favorite sport in Marco's school? Why? Write your answer on another paper.

Using New Words

A. Write the word that makes sense in each sentence.

envelope	figured	circle	fountain
mystery	refreshment cart	solve	view

1. It is something that is hard to know. It is a _____ .

2. You thought hard about it.

   You _____ out what it is.

3. Here are five little mysteries. Can you

   _____ them?

4. It is not a square. It is round like a ring. It is a ___ .

5. It is in the park. Water splashes in it. It is a ___ .

6. It holds a letter. It is made of paper. It is an ___ .

7. It is an open space that people look at. It is a ___ .

8. It is a wagon holding snacks and drinks. It is a ___ .

B. On another paper, write a mystery of your own.

The Treasure Hunt

A. Write one or more words on each line to finish the story
about ''The Treasure Hunt.''

| Marita | park | stone bench | tickets | zoo |

In this story, Mr. Ortero made up a mystery for Jenny, Tommy,

_____

Mike, and _____ . Mr. Ortero hid a treasure

_____

----

in the _____ . But where did he hide it? And

what was it?

Marita's clue told her that the treasure was near a fountain. Jenny's

clue told them to look near the merry-go-round. Tommy's clue said

they should look for a fountain that had a view of the

_____

_____ . Mike's clue told them that they

_____

----

would find the treasure near a _____ .

Using all the clues, the children found the treasure. It was a set of

_____

----

free _____ for the park festival!

B. Pretend that you have hidden a treasure somewhere
around your house. On another paper, write three clues
to help others find the treasure.

Context Clues

REMEMBER: The words and sentences around an unknown word can help you figure out the meaning of that unknown word.

A. Read each sentence. Think about the meaning of the underlined word. Then circle the letter of the correct answer.

1. Mr. Ortero was very <u>humorous</u>. People thought he was funny.
   A person who is <u>humorous</u> would enjoy ___ .
   a. being alone   **b.** telling jokes

2. The <u>monument</u>, a big stone carving of a man on a horse, was in the middle of the park.
   A <u>monument</u> is made to ___ .
   a. help people remember an   **b.** give animals food in
   important person or happening   winter

3. Tom was <u>baffled</u> by his clue. Jenny did not understand hers either.
   A person who is <u>baffled</u> ___ .
   a. is very forgetful   **b.** has a hard time understanding

4. The park's <u>flora</u> included trees, bushes, and flowers.
   To buy <u>flora</u>, you would go to a ___ .
   a. gardening shop   **b.** bookstore

B. On another paper, write your own sentence using one of the underlined words in Part A. In the sentence, show you know what the word means.

NAME _____

Predicting Outcomes

> **REMEMBER:** When you **predict,** you make a guess about what will happen in a story. Use story clues and what you know to make a good prediction.

A. Read each paragraph. Write what might happen next.

1. Marita walked to the festival. She saw her friends at the refreshment cart. She wanted her free drink, too. Marita will

   _____
   -
   _____ .

   push her way in   wait for her turn   go home

2. At the festival, the children talk about how they helped each other find the treasure. Then Tommy finds out he has left his free ticket at home.   The children will

   _____
   -
   _____ .

   leave Tommy outside   loan Tommy money   go on a ride

B. On another paper, write a sentence that tells about what might happen next in the second story. Use what you already know about the story.

Words with *au, aw*

> **REMEMBER:** The letters *au* and *aw* can stand for the vowel sound you hear in *pause* and *jaw*.

A. Write the answer to each of the riddles.

| because | claws | fawn | hawk | lawn | yawn |

1. I am something people do when they are sleepy. What am I?

_____

2. I am a little deer. What am I?

_____

3. I am what you say when people ask you why. What word am I?

_____

4. I am sharp tips on a cat's toes. What am I?

_____

5. I am a bird with very sharp eyes. What am I?

_____

6. I am the grass in front of a house. What am I?

_____

B. On another paper, draw a picture for one of the words you wrote. Write a sentence about your picture.

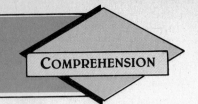

NAME

Main Idea/Details

> **REMEMBER:** The **main idea** is the most important idea in a paragraph. Supporting details tell more about the main idea.

A. Underline the sentence that tells the main idea of each paragraph. Then write one more detail that goes with the main idea.

1. It is a good idea for people to work together. People can share each other's ideas. They can finish the work more quickly. Also, they can have fun working together.

_____

_____

_____

_____

_____

2. Most children love to go to park festivals. There is music and dancing. There are fun games to play. Everyone can have a good time.

_____

_____

_____

_____

B. On another paper, draw a picture of one of the paragraphs in Part A. Write a sentence that tells the main idea of your picture. Write a sentence that tells one detail.

Using New Words

A. Write the word that means the same thing as the underlined words.

faraway islands maps possible routes sailors valuable voyages

1. It takes a lot of work to plan <u>long boat trips</u>.

   _____

2. First you need to get <u>drawings that show places</u>.

   _____

3. Then you need to plan <u>ways to go</u>.

   _____

4. You may go to a land that is <u>a long way off</u>.

   _____

5. Sometimes people sail to <u>lands with water all around them</u>.

   _____

6. Some may hope to find things that are <u>worth a lot</u>.

   _____

7. Sometimes <u>people who sail</u> find treasure.

   _____

8. Anything is <u>able to be done</u> on long sea voyages.

   _____

B. Pretend that you are going on a sea voyage. On another paper, write a story about it.

NAME _____

Christopher Columbus's Voyage

A. Write one or more words on each line to finish the story about "Christopher Columbus's Voyage."

America	Asia	five weeks	Italy	Queen of Spain

This story tells about the life of Christopher Columbus. When he _____ was a boy in Genoa, _____ , he loved to spend time talking to sailors. As he grew older, he went on voyages and learned to sail ships and read maps. Christopher loved the sea.

When he became a man, Christopher Columbus wanted to sail to _____ . He decided to take a _____ new route. The _____ gave him the money for his voyage.

The voyage was long and hard. His sailors wanted Columbus to _____ turn back, but he would not. After _____ at sea, they saw land. Columbus and his sailors had landed near what we now call _____ .

B. On another paper, write two sentences that tell what you think happened when Columbus's ships reached land.

Words with *ew*

REMEMBER: The letters *ew* can stand for the vowel sounds in *flew* and *few*.

A. Underline each word that has the same vowel sound you hear in either *flew* or *few*. Then write each underlined word on the line.

Christopher Columbus grew up in a small city near the sea. A few of the sailors would tell him about their voyages. They told about how the wind blew in storms at sea. They knew about many faraway places. They drew their routes for him on their maps. The time flew by as he listened. Columbus could hardly wait to travel to new places himself.

_____

_____

_____   _____

_____   _____

_____   _____

_____   _____

B. Are there faraway places you would like to visit? On another paper, write three sentences that tell how you could find out more about these places.

COMPREHENSION

Predicting Outcomes

> **REMEMBER:** When you **predict,** you make a guess about what will happen in a story. Use story clues and what you know to make a good prediction.

A. Read the sentences. Guess what will happen next. Circle your guess. Then write it.

1. A sailor looked at his maps. He picked a faraway place. He put food and other things on his ship. He asked other sailors to go with him. What will happen next?

   The sailor will sell the boat.   The sailor will lose his map.

   The sailor will leave on a long voyage.

   _____

   -

   _____

2. A sailor was on a voyage. Suddenly, the sky grew dark. The wind blew. The ship rocked. Black clouds were everywhere.
   What will happen next?
   The sailor will find a treasure.   A storm will come up.

   The sun will come out.

   _____

   -

   _____

B. Pick one group of sentences from Part A. On another paper, draw a picture that shows what will happen next. Write a sentence that tells why you think so.

NAME _____

Long Word Decoding

> **REMEMBER:** When you try to read a long word, look for words and word parts you know.

A. Circle the words or word parts you know. Underline the vowel letters.

staple   locate   metal   harmless   wander

B. Write one of the words in Part A to answer each question.

1. Which word describes iron and gold?

_____

2. Which word means "find"?

_____

3. Which word means "roam or go about aimlessly"?

_____

4. Which word names a thin piece of metal that fastens papers together?

_____

5. Which word means the opposite of *harmful*?

_____

C. On another paper, use two of the words you wrote in Part B to write a sentence of your own.

Checkpoint

Read the story. Then fill in the circle next to the correct answer.

Kids can do a lot of things to help out in their towns. Finding a way to make a few dollars can help buy the new things the town needs. In my town, we needed a new bench for the park.

A whole crew of kids on my block threw a street fair. We made a big sign telling people to come. The sign also said that there would be a prize. Then we made food for people to eat as they played games and heard music. The people paid to eat and play and listen. Everybody had a good time, and the morning flew by.

At noon, we planned to tell who won the prize. I had the prize box on my lap when Jimmy's dog came by. From inside the box, he heard a mew. Jimmy's dog gave a loud bark, and, before we knew it, our prize sprang out of the box.

We knew the prize would be the best part of the fair. We just didn't know how very exciting it would be!

1. What prize will the winner probably get?
   a) a cat
   b) a bird
   c) a bunny

2. Which sentence from the story helped you decide what the prize was?
   a) The people paid to eat and play and listen.
   b) From inside the box, he heard a mew.
   c) We knew the prize would be the best part of the fair.

3. What might happen next in the story?
   a) Jimmy's dog went home as fast as he could.
   b) Jimmy's dog chased the cat.
   c) The fair ended soon.

4. What do you know that helped you guess what might happen next?
   a) Dogs often chase cats.
   b) Cats mew.
   c) Everybody likes dogs.

5. Which word has the same vowel sound as the underlined letters in *fl<u>ew</u>*?
   a) thumb   c) threw
   b) throw   d) throne

6. Which word has the same vowel sound as the underlined letters in *m<u>ew</u>*?
   a) flow   c) flower
   b) few   d) fur

7. Which word has the same vowel sound as the underlined letters in *bl<u>ew</u>*?
   a) knew   c) nut
   b) now   d) nurse

8. Which word has the same vowel sound as the underlined letters in *fl<u>ew</u>*?
   a) know   c) now
   b) nothing   d) new

Vocabulary Review

Fill in the circle next to the word that best fits in the sentence.

1. Alice's ___ is 15 Woodcut Lane.
   (a) cousin   (b) address   (c) mystery   (d) nickname

2. My ___ will spend a week with my family.
   (a) snowflake   (b) fountain   (c) frames   (d) cousin

3. The skater made a ___ on the ice.
   (a) circle   (b) mystery   (c) snowman   (d) frames

4. Dad looked at the ___ to find out how to get to the city.
   (a) goal   (b) office   (c) voyages   (d) maps

5. Mom goes to her ___ every morning.
   (a) office   (b) windshield   (c) goalie   (d) maps

6. Paul ___ a glass of milk for his little sister.
   (a) promise   (b) poured   (c) challenge   (d) figured

7. Karen made us ___ not to tell the secret.
   (a) poured   (b) slid   (c) promise   (d) solve

8. Rob chose blue ___ for his new eyeglasses.

   (a) sailors   (b) voyages   (c) maps   (d) frames

9. Jan made one ___ in the soccer game.

   (a) goal   (b) office   (c) address   (d) cousin

10. Joe wrote Nan's address on the ___ before he mailed the letter.

   (a) mystery   (b) envelope   (c) score   (d) cousin

11. Carrie knew two ___ home from school.

   (a) rules   (b) wipers   (c) routes   (d) islands

12. Ken played ___ in the soccer game.

   (a) goalie   (b) score   (c) circle   (d) snowflake

13. The ___ at the end of the ball game was 3 to 1.

   (a) refreshment cart   (b) view   (c) sports   (d) score

14. The ___ worked on a big ship.

   (a) frames   (b) voyages   (c) envelope   (d) sailors

15. The spaceship made two ___ to the moon.

   (a) score   (b) routes   (c) office   (d) voyages

NAME _____

Unit Wrap-Up

Write the answer to each question.

1. In "Watch Out, Ronald Morgan!" Ronald's new glasses helped him be himself in many new ways. Did Dandelion's new clothes help him to be himself? Why or why not?

_____

- -

_____

- -

_____

2. Sam in "Soccer Sam" knew that the team would win if everyone worked together. How did the children in "The Treasure Hunt" work together? Did they win in the end?

_____

- -

_____

- -

_____

3. Which character in "Soccer Sam" came to America? What did he do in America to put his best foot forward?

_____

- -

_____

- -

_____

What Interests Me

Circle the pictures that show things you like to read about.
Use the chart to find out which books you would enjoy.

1	2	3	4	BOOK LIST
★	★		★	*There's a Train Going by My Window* by Wendy Kesselman
		★	★	*Ming Lo Moves the Mountain* by Arnold Lobel
★			★	*This Is Edinburgh* by M. Sasek
	★	★		*The Cow Who Fell in the Canal* by Phyllis Krasilovsky
★	★			*The Red Balloon* by Albert Lamorisse

NAME _____

My Book List

Name of Book

_____

- - - - - - - - - - - - - - - - - - - -

_____

Author

_____

- - - - - - - - - - - - - - - - - - - -

_____

Name of Book

_____

- - - - - - - - - - - - - - - - - - - -

_____

Author

_____

- - - - - - - - - - - - - - - - - - - -

_____

Words with *ld, lk, mb, mn*

> **REMEMBER:** The letters *ld, lk, mb,* and *mn* can stand for the sounds you hear at the end of *could, talk, comb,* and *column.*

A. Read each sentence and the words. Write the word that makes sense and has the sound you hear at the end of *could, talk, comb,* or *column.*

_____

1. Bert _____ not pay for an airplane ticket.

     might   stalk   could

_____

2. So he decided to _____ around the world.

     comb   walk   come

_____

3. Bert's legs felt _____ when he returned home.

     numb   hymn   heavy

4. A woman wrote a story about Bert's walk in a newspaper

_____

_____ .

     story   column   talk

B. Choose one of the words with *ld, lk, mb,* or *mn* you did not use in Part A. On another paper, write a sentence about Bert, using that word.

NAME _____

Words with *eigh*

> **REMEMBER:** The letters *eigh* can stand for the vowel sound you hear in *eight*.

A. Read the story. Underline each word that has the same vowel sound you hear in *eight*. Then write the words on the lines.

> I rode my horse to a faraway place. I knew I was there when I heard my horse neigh. I climbed off his back and looked around. I saw a gold rock that weighed five pounds. Maybe I'll stay here for eighty years. But when I go home, I'll still be eight!

_____

_____

_____

_____

_____

_____

B. Imagine that you are going on a trip to a faraway place. On another paper, write two sentences about the trip. Use two words with *eigh*.

130 "The Story of Paul Bunyan"   Vowel Digraph *ei (gh)* /ā/

Using New Words

A. Write the word to answer each question.

cleared	loggers	lumber	mightiest
ox	sawmill	strength	wheat

1. We are the people who cut down the trees. Who are we?

_____

- -

_____

2. This is the animal that may help us move the trees. What is it?

_____

- -

_____

3. This is a place where saws are used to cut trees. What is it?

_____

- -

_____

4. This is how the land is after the trees are gone. How is it?

_____

- -

_____

5. This is what it takes to cut and move the trees. What is it?

_____

- -

_____

6. This word means the same as "the strongest of all." Which word is it?

_____

- -

_____

7. This is what the trees are made into. What is this?

_____

- -

_____

8. Farmers can plant this after the trees are gone. What is it?

_____

- -

_____

B. On another paper, draw a picture that shows something that loggers do. Write a sentence to go with your picture.

THE STORY OF
PAUL BUNYAN

A. Write one or more words on each line to tell about "The Story of Paul Bunyan."

Babe	forest	Maine	Mississippi River	Paul Bunyan

This story is about a time long ago when our country was one

_____

great _____ . At that time, mighty loggers worked

to clear the land. The mightiest logger of all was

_____

_____ .

Paul was kind and gentle, but he was as strong as a hundred men.

_____

He dug the _____ in

_____

one afternoon. Even as a baby in Kennebunkport, _____ ,

Paul kicked so hard he moved a few barns.

One winter, Paul noticed a big blue ox tail sticking out of the

_____

snow. He called the ox _____ , and they became

great friends. Together, they cleared the land.

B. On another paper, write two sentences about Paul
Bunyan. In one, tell something that could happen. In the
other one, tell something that could *not* happen. Draw a
picture to go with each sentence.

Prefixes *re-*, *un-*

> **REMEMBER:** The prefix *re-* means "again" or "back."
> The prefix *un-* means "not."

A. Write the word that means the same as the underlined words.

1. Paul liked the book. He decided to <u>read</u> it <u>again</u>.

   _____

   -

   _____

2. There were too many trees in Kansas. The farmers there

   _____

   -

   were <u>not happy</u>. _____

   _____

   -

3. They were <u>not able</u> to grow much wheat. _____

4. After Paul cleared the land, he <u>turned back</u> home.

   _____

   -

   _____

5. Paul and Babe went deep into the woods. Where they are now is

   _____

   -

   <u>not known</u>. _____

B. On another paper, write a sentence about something Paul
Bunyan might have done. Use as many words with the
prefix *re-* or *un-* as you can.

Synonyms

> **REMEMBER: Synonyms** are words that mean about the same thing. *Big* and *large* are synonyms.

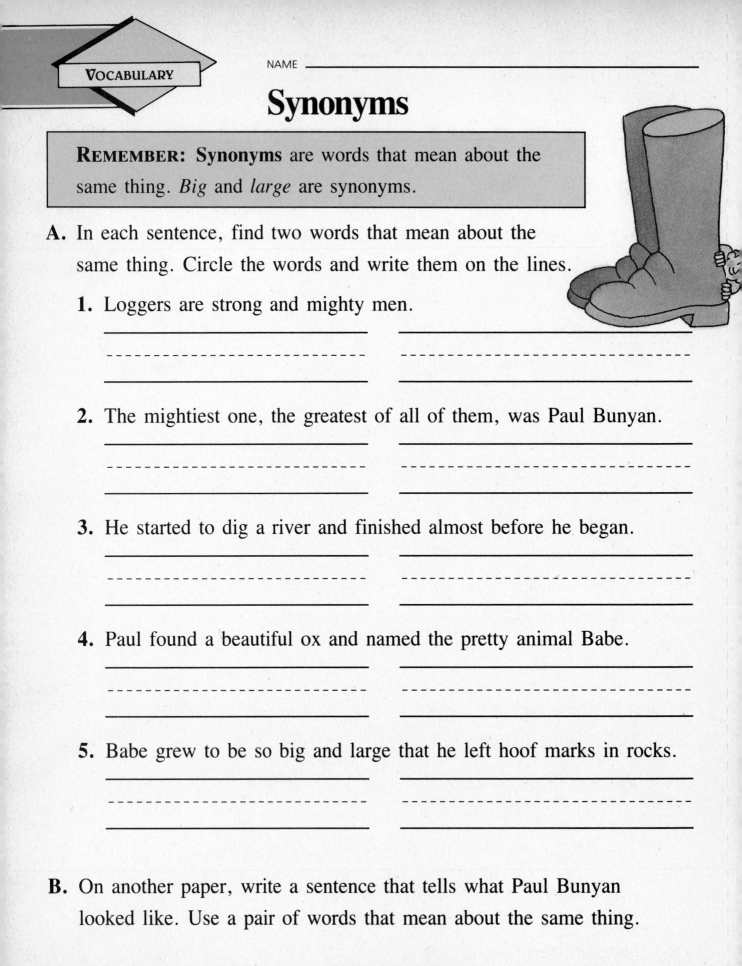

A. In each sentence, find two words that mean about the same thing. Circle the words and write them on the lines.

1. Loggers are strong and mighty men.

_____   _____

2. The mightiest one, the greatest of all of them, was Paul Bunyan.

_____   _____

3. He started to dig a river and finished almost before he began.

_____   _____

4. Paul found a beautiful ox and named the pretty animal Babe.

_____   _____

5. Babe grew to be so big and large that he left hoof marks in rocks.

_____   _____

B. On another paper, write a sentence that tells what Paul Bunyan looked like. Use a pair of words that mean about the same thing.

Words with *eigh*

REMEMBER: The letters *eigh* can stand for the vowel sound you hear in *eight*.

A. Circle the word that makes sense in each sentence and has the vowel sound as in *eight*. Then write the word on the line.

_____

1. Paul Bunyan _____ 105 pounds when he was a baby.

   was   weighed   eighty

_____

2. The _____ of his beard was forty-six pounds.

   weight   size   neigh

_____

3. I wonder how heavy he was when he was _____ .

   born   neigh   eight

_____

4. Paul's ox Babe would _____ a lot, too.

   eight   weigh   eat

_____

5. Babe was as strong as _____ men.

   weighed   seventy   eighty

_____

6. Paul could cut down _____ trees at once.

   freight   eighteen   fifty

B. On another paper, write a sentence about Babe.

NAME _____

Words with *ld*, *lk*, *mb*, *mn*

REMEMBER: The letters *ld*, *lk*, *mb*, and *mn* can stand for the sounds you hear at the end of *could*, *talk*, *comb*, and *column*.

A. Write words under the right letters to finish the chart.

| column | could | lamb | solemn | thumb |
| comb | folk | should | talk | would |

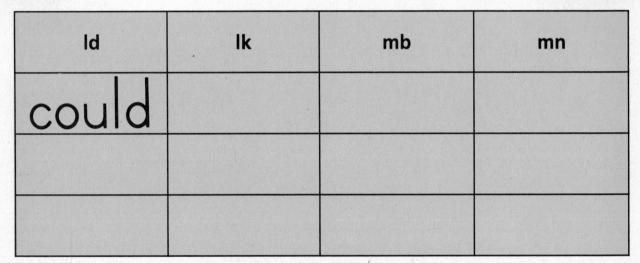

ld	lk	mb	mn
could			

B. Write a sentence that tells what you would do if you could meet Paul Bunyan. Use words that end with the letters *ld*, *lk*, *mb*, or *mn* in your sentence.

_____

- -

_____

- -

_____

C. On another paper, draw a picture to go with the sentence you wrote in Part B.

Characterization

> **REMEMBER:** To understand a character in a story, think about what the character says and does. Also think about how the character speaks and acts.

A. Read the sentences. Write the word that tells about each person.

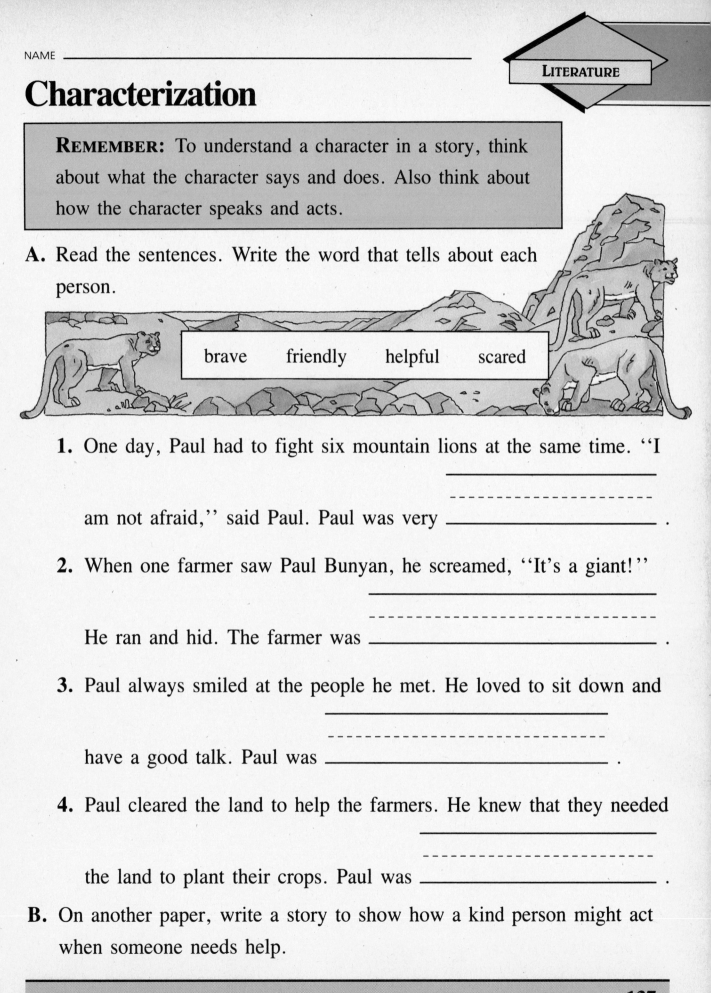

| brave | friendly | helpful | scared |

1. One day, Paul had to fight six mountain lions at the same time. "I

   _____

   am not afraid," said Paul. Paul was very _____ .

2. When one farmer saw Paul Bunyan, he screamed, "It's a giant!"

   _____

   He ran and hid. The farmer was _____ .

3. Paul always smiled at the people he met. He loved to sit down and

   _____

   have a good talk. Paul was _____ .

4. Paul cleared the land to help the farmers. He knew that they needed

   _____

   the land to plant their crops. Paul was _____ .

B. On another paper, write a story to show how a kind person might act when someone needs help.

NAME _____

Using New Words

A. Read the word in the circle. Then read the word
meanings. Write the word that matches each meaning.

| dough except hotel jokes journal pizza talker yeast |

_____   _____
- - - - - - - - - - - - - - - - - - -   - - - - - - - - - - - - - - - - - - -
_____

mix for making bread or pie crust   a thing that makes bread rise

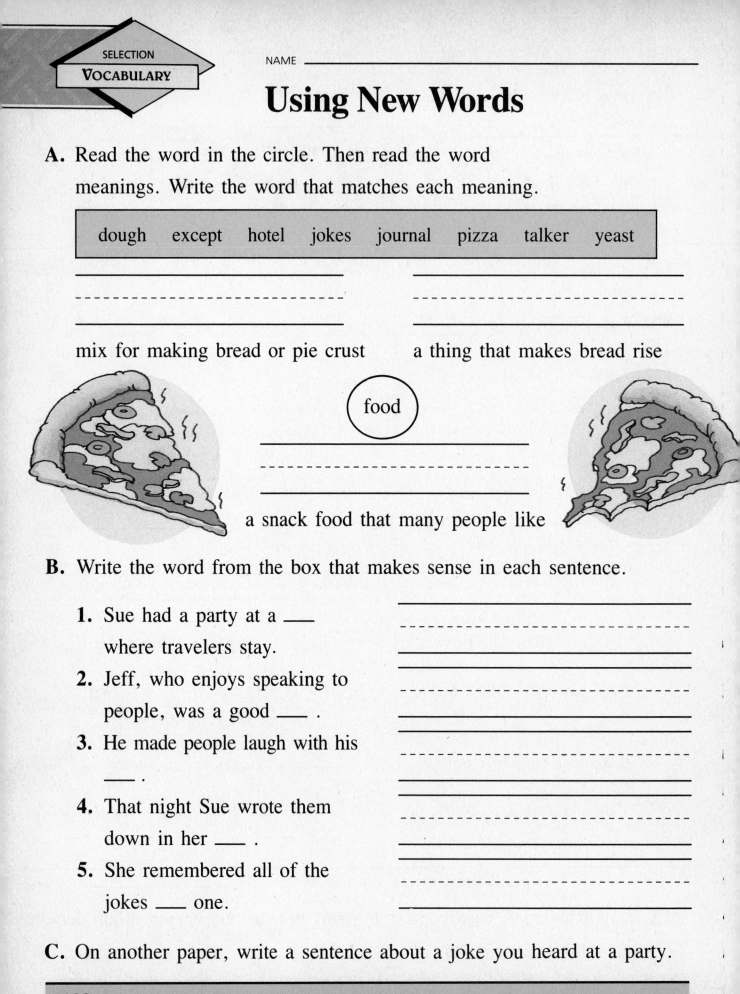

(food)

_____
- - - - - - - - - - - - - - - - - - -

a snack food that many people like

B. Write the word from the box that makes sense in each sentence.

1. Sue had a party at a ___
   where travelers stay.
2. Jeff, who enjoys speaking to
   people, was a good ___ .
3. He made people laugh with his
   ___ .
4. That night Sue wrote them
   down in her ___ .
5. She remembered all of the
   jokes ___ one.

_____
- - - - - - - - - - - - - - - - - - -
_____
_____
- - - - - - - - - - - - - - - - - - -
_____
_____
- - - - - - - - - - - - - - - - - - -
_____
_____
- - - - - - - - - - - - - - - - - - -
_____
_____
- - - - - - - - - - - - - - - - - - -
_____

C. On another paper, write a sentence about a joke you heard at a party.

A SMOOTH MOVE

A. Write one or more words on each line to finish the story about "A Smooth Move."

| at a hotel | Gus | missed | new friends | teacher |

_____

This story is about _____ , who started a journal when his family moved from Oregon to Washington, D.C. Gus and his mother flew to Washington, D.C. They stayed

_____

_____ . When the furniture came, they moved into their new house.

_____

Gus liked his new _____ . He

_____

soon made many _____ . Gus was happy with his new home and school. But he still

_____

_____ his old friends in Oregon.

B. Imagine you are Gus. On another paper, write a letter to a friend in Oregon about your new home and friends.

NAME _____

Spelling Changes

> **REMEMBER:** When a word ends with *f* or *fe*, you usually change the *f* to *v* before adding *-s* or *-es*.

A. Use the underlined word to finish the second sentence. Change *f* to *v* and add *–s* or *–es*.

1. Gus cleared off the <u>shelf</u> in his room. His mother cleared off

   _____

   -

   the _____ in the rest of the house.

2. He packed his little brother's fork and <u>knife</u>. His mother packed the

   _____

   -

   other _____ .

3. Gus raked up every <u>leaf</u> in the yard. He must have raked

   _____

   -

   those _____ for hours!

4. Gus had never worked so hard in his <u>life</u>. He and his mother had

   _____

   -

   never worked so hard in their _____ .

B. On another paper, write the underlined words. Then beside each one, write the word that means more than one.

Prefixes re-, un-

> **REMEMBER:** The prefix *re-* means "again" or "back."
> The prefix *un-* means "not."

A. Write a word on each line that means the same as the
words under the line. The word you write should begin
with *un-* or *re-*.

1. The moving van broke down. Mother said that it had been an

   _____

   -

   _____ van.

               not lucky

2. The men fixed the van. They took out the broken parts and

   _____

   -

   _____ them with new ones.

          placed back

3. What an _____ start this was, Gus

thought.   not happy

4. Then his mother told him a funny joke.

   _____

   -

   Gus _____ the joke to his new friends.

          told again

B. On another paper, write a new sentence that tells about
Gus and his move. Use a word that starts with *re-* or *un-*
in your sentence.

NAME _____

Characterization

> **REMEMBER:** To understand a character in a story, think about what the character says and does. Also think about how the character speaks and acts.

A. Write the words that tell what each person might have done.

1. Gus was funny. He liked to

_____

- -

_____ .

fly kites   tell jokes   draw pictures

2. Gus's friend, Paul, was very shy. He liked to

_____

- -

_____ .

play ball   read alone   tell jokes

3. Gus's friend, Anna, was brave. She liked to

_____

- -

_____ .

try new things   save money   wash dishes

4. Gus's friend, Nelson, was helpful. He liked to

_____

- -

_____ .

wash dishes   eat pizza   write stories

B. On another paper, write two sentences about a new thing you would like to do.

Synonyms

> **REMEMBER: Synonyms** are words that mean about the same thing. *Big* and *large* are synonyms.

A. Read each sentence. Write the word that means about the same thing as the underlined word.

1. All the furniture was in a moving <u>van.</u>

    _____

    place   train   truck

2. Gus <u>liked</u> the hotel they stayed in.

    _____

    loved   found   worked

3. Gus's new school was a <u>high</u> building.

    _____

    short   dark   tall

4. Mom said the move had been <u>difficult.</u>

    _____

    interesting   slow   hard

5. Gus thought that the move had been <u>easy.</u>

    _____

    careful   silly   smooth

B. On another paper, write about a family's move. In your sentences, use one of the synonym pairs from Part A.

Checkpoint

Read the story. Then fill in the circle next to the correct answer.

When I was eight, we moved from the city to a small town in Maine. At first it was <u>difficult</u> for me. I'm not the kind of kid who can walk up and talk to a strange person. People say I'm the solemn sort. For a long time, the only people I knew were our neighbors.

Then one day I was out walking and I heard a sound about eighty feet off the road. I stopped because I just had to know what it was. I found an old dog with his paw caught in a trap. "Hurt your thumb, old boy?" I said. My mom helped me get him out.

That evening we found out whose dog he was. We took him home. You should have seen the kid's face when he got his dog back! After that, he introduced me to all his friends. Now I don't have to worry about talking to people I don't know. I know just about every kid in town!

1. Which word tells what the boy in the story was like when he first moved?
   (a) lazy
   (c) shy
   (b) friendly

2. Which sentence helped you know what he was like?
   (a) I'm not the kind of kid who can walk up and talk to a strange person.
   (b) At first it was difficult for me.
   (c) When I was eight, we moved from the city to a small town in Maine.

3. Which word means about the same as the underlined word *difficult*?
   (a) easy
   (c) different
   (b) hard

4. Which word has the same vowel sound as the underlined letters in *eight*?
   (a) wake
   (c) want
   (b) went
   (d) walk

5. Which word has the same sound as the underlined letters in *cou<u>ld</u>*?
   (a) tall
   (c) helped
   (b) walk
   (d) should

6. Which word has the same sound as the underlined letters in *co<u>mb</u>*?
   (a) dip
   (c) cone
   (b) cub
   (d) thumb

7. Which word has the same sound as the underlined letters in *ta<u>lk</u>*?
   (a) walk
   (c) want
   (b) wall
   (d) wild

8. Which word has the same sound as the underlined letters in *colu<u>mn</u>*?
   (a) sun
   (c) sand
   (b) solemn
   (d) sold

NAME _____

Cause / Effect

REMEMBER: Use signal words, story clues, and what you already know to figure out which events caused other events to happen.

A. Read each sentence. Draw a line under the part that tells why something happened. Then write what happened on the line.

1. Gus and his family had to move because Dad got a new job.

_____

_ _

_____

2. Gus got a good report card. Therefore, he was very happy.

_____

_ _

_____

3. Paul told a funny joke, so Gus laughed.

_____

_ _

_____

4. Gus was sad because he missed his old friends.

_____

_ _

_____

B. On another paper, write a sentence that tells about something that happened to you. Use *because, so,* or *therefore* in your sentence to tell why it happened.

Using New Words

A. Write each word on the line where it makes sense.

bowed	fork	marry	ordered	restaurant	utensils	waiter

1. You are going out to eat. You are going to a

_____

- -

_____ .

2. You tell someone what you want. You tell a

_____

- -

_____ .

3. Maybe the waiter did this after he took your order. He

_____

- -

_____ .

4. This is the food you asked for. It is what you

_____

- -

_____ .

5. You use these to eat your food. They are

_____

- -

_____ .

6. You might drop this and have to ask for a new one. It is a

_____

- -

_____ .

7. A wedding party is planned. A man and a woman will

_____

- -

_____ .

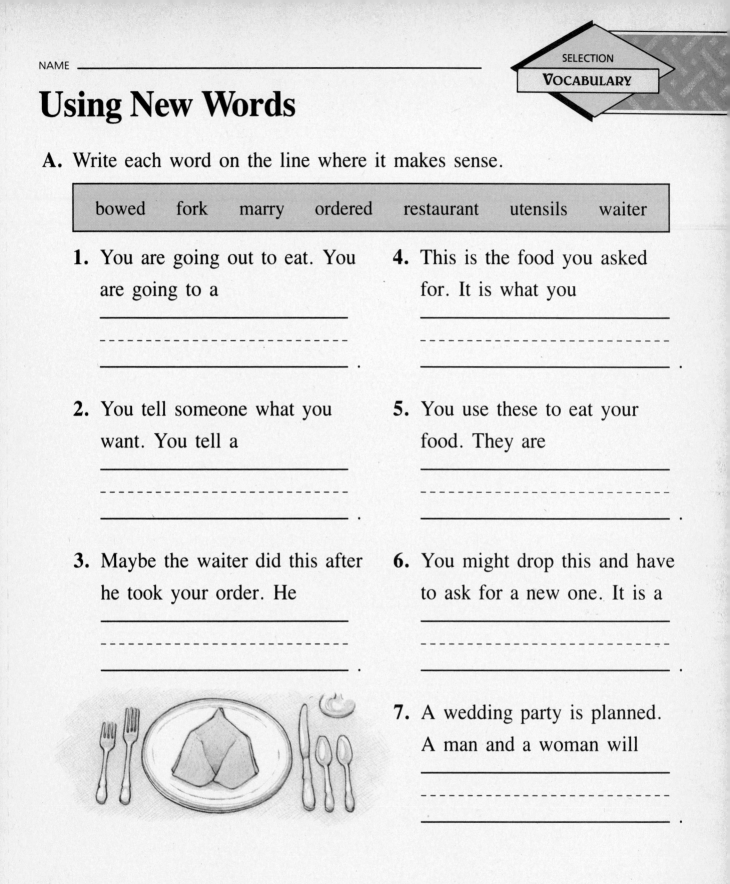

B. On another paper, draw a picture of some people eating in a restaurant. Write two sentences that go with your picture. Use as many story words as you can.

How My Parents Learned to Eat

A. Write one or more words on each line to finish the story
about "How My Parents Learned to Eat."

both	chopsticks	Great Uncle	learned to eat	Yokohama

This story is about two people from different countries. Each

_____

- -

_____ in a new way. John was

_____

- -

stationed as an American sailor in _____ ,

Japan. That was where he met Aiko, his future wife.

    John was used to eating with a knife and fork. Aiko could eat

_____

- -

with _____ only. Each thought they
would look silly trying to eat in a new way.

    John decided to learn to eat with chopsticks. Aiko learned to use a

_____

- -

knife and fork from _____ . Finally
John and Aiko ate together. They decided that when they got married

_____

- - - - - - - - - - - - -

they would eat _____ ways.

B. Think of ideas for a new kind of eating utensil. On
another paper, draw a picture of it. Under the picture,
write a sentence about how you would use it.

Spelling Changes

> **REMEMBER:** When a word ends with *f* or *fe*, you
> usually change the *f* to *v* before adding *-s* or *-es*.

A. Read each sentence. Circle the word in which the *f* was
changed to *v* before *-s* or *-es* was added. Then write the
word as it was before the change.

1. All their lives, my parents
   have talked about how they met.

   _____

2. Our shelves hold pictures of
   the restaurant where they met.

   _____

3. My mother did not know about
   eating with forks and knives.

   _____

4. My mother still wears the
   scarves my father gave her.

   _____

5. Like other husbands and
   wives, my parents like to eat at
   the restaurant where they met.

   _____

B. On another paper, rewrite two sentences in Part A using
the words you wrote.

NAME _____

Cause / Effect

> **REMEMBER:** Use signal words, story clues, and what you already know to figure out which events caused other events to happen.

A. Circle the sentence that tells what happened. Then write the sentence that tells why it happened.

1. My father did not know how to use chopsticks.
He did not ask my mother to dinner.

_____
- -
_____

2. My mother was sad.
My father had not called.

_____
- -
_____

3. My mother wanted to learn how to use a fork and knife.
My mother visited Great Uncle.

_____
- -
_____
- -
_____

B. On another paper, write a pair of sentences about something that happened when you went out to eat. One sentence should tell what happened. The other sentence should tell why it happened. Use words like *because, so,* or *therefore*.

Words with *eigh*

> **REMEMBER:** The letters *eigh* can stand for the vowel sound you hear in *eight*.

A. Read the story. Underline each word in which the letters *eigh* stand for the vowel sound you hear in *eight*. Write the words.

Everybody eats, no matter if they are eighteen or eighty. But people eat in different ways. Americans eat in a different way from their British neighbors.

All animals eat, too. Horses neigh when they are hungry. They must get hungry pulling a sleigh or a load of freight.

Chomp Chomp

_____   _____

_____   _____

_____   _____

B. On another paper, write two sentences about numbers. Use at least one word with *eigh* in it.

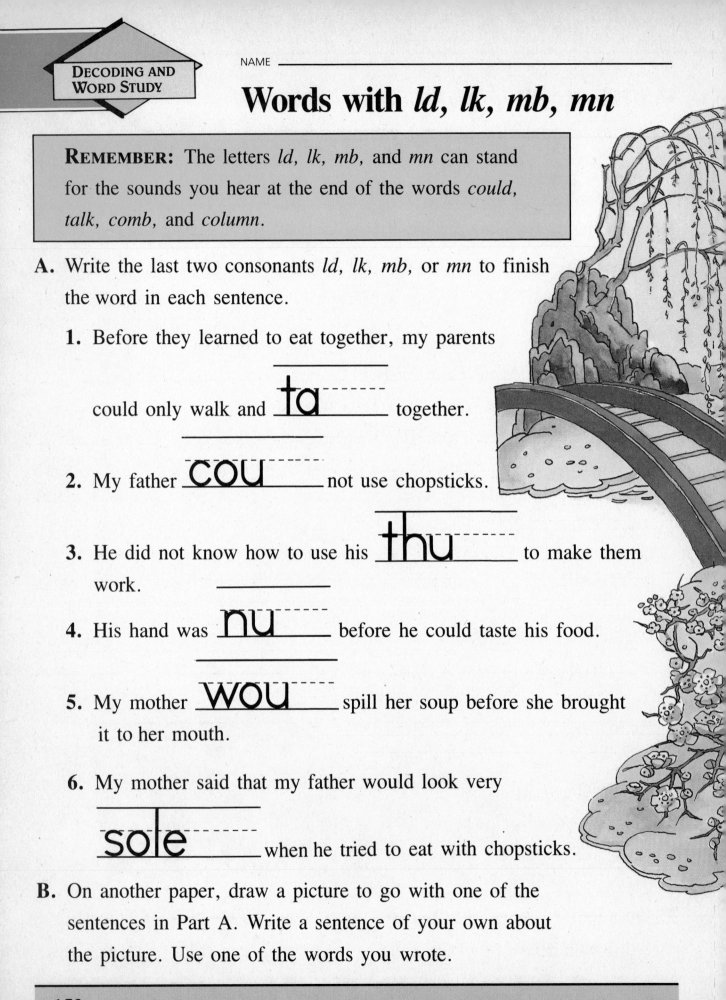

Words with *ld, lk, mb, mn*

REMEMBER: The letters *ld, lk, mb,* and *mn* can stand
for the sounds you hear at the end of the words *could,*
talk, comb, and *column.*

A. Write the last two consonants *ld, lk, mb,* or *mn* to finish
the word in each sentence.

1. Before they learned to eat together, my parents

   could only walk and **ta**_____ together.

2. My father **cou**_____ not use chopsticks.

3. He did not know how to use his **thu**_____ to make them
   work.

4. His hand was **nu**_____ before he could taste his food.

5. My mother **wou**_____ spill her soup before she brought
   it to her mouth.

6. My mother said that my father would look very

   sole_____ when he tried to eat with chopsticks.

B. On another paper, draw a picture to go with one of the
sentences in Part A. Write a sentence of your own about
the picture. Use one of the words you wrote.

Words with *t (fortune)*

> **REMEMBER:** The letter *t* can stand for the sound you hear in the middle of *fortune*.

A. Read each sentence. Underline one word with the letter *t* that stands for the sound you hear in the middle of *fortune*. Then write the word on the line.

1. My parents had the good fortune to meet in Japan.

2. They both wished they could have a future together.

3. They knew their life together would be a mixture of American

   and Japanese ways. _____

4. They each could picture how nice their life would be.

5. Learning to live in two worlds would become second

   nature to my parents. _____

B. On another paper, write two sentences about food you eat without using a knife, fork, or spoon.

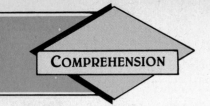

NAME _____

Word Referents

REMEMBER: Some words can stand for the names of people, places, or things.

A. Read each group of sentences. Circle the words that each underlined word stands for. Then finish each sentence with "which one," "which ones," or "where."

1. My parents like to tell the story of how they learned to eat. <u>That</u> is my favorite.

_____
- - - - - - - - - - - - - - - - -

That tells _____ .

2. A waiter taught my father to eat with chopsticks. <u>These</u> were hard for him to use.

_____

- - - - - - - - - - - - - - - - -

These tells _____ .

3. My mother knew people ate with different utensils in America. She wanted to be able to eat <u>there</u>.

_____

- - - - - - - - - - - - - - - - -

There tells _____ .

4. "It is so different in Japan," she thought. "It is so easy to eat <u>here</u>."

_____
- - - - - - - - - - - - - - - - -

Here tells _____ .

5. Great Uncle taught my mother how to use English utensils. It was hard for her to use <u>those</u>.

_____

- - - - - - - - - - - - - - - - -

Those tells _____ .

6. I have told you the story of how my parents learned to eat. Don't you think <u>it</u> is good?

_____

- - - - - - - - - - - - - - - - -

It tells _____ .

B. On another paper, write a pair of sentences about the mother in Part A using English utensils. Use a word that tells "which one" or "where."

Using New Words

A. Write the words to finish the story.

| cartoons | characters | popular | published | statue |

_____

_____ are fun to read. They are

_____

_____ in the newspaper every day. My

favorite is about a boy and his dog. I like

_____

these _____ the most. They are the

_____

most _____ with children my age.

_____

I saw a _____ of the boy and his dog. It

was made out of clay. I wish I had one to put in my room. The

_____

_____ have become my friends.

B. On another paper, draw a picture of your favorite
cartoon character. Use some of the story words to write
a sentence to go with your picture.

NAME _____

LEE BENNETT HOPKINS INTERVIEWS
Betsy and Giulio Maestro

A. Write one or more words on each line to finish the sentences about
"Lee Bennett Hopkins Interviews Betsy and Giulio Maestro."

Betsy and Giulio	Brooklyn	cartoon characters
pictures	together	

This story is about _____

_____

Maestro. Betsy grew up in _____ , New
York, where she loved to read books. Giulio grew up in Greenwich
Village. He always wanted to _____

draw _____ .

Betsy loved to write books for children. She knew that Giulio

could draw wonderful _____ to go in her
books. Since they met, Betsy and Giulio have worked

_____ on many books for children. Many
of the Maestros' books are in the library for children to enjoy.

B. On another paper, draw a picture that goes with a story you like. Write
the name of the story.

Spelling Changes

> **REMEMBER:** When a word ends with *f* or *fe*, you usually change the *f* to *v* before adding *-s* or *-es*.

A. Read each pair of sentences. Change the underlined word to mean more than one. Then finish the second sentence with your new word.

1. When Betsy writes, she is as busy as an <u>elf</u>. When she and Giulio

_____

- - - - - - - - - - - - - - - - -

work together, they work like _____ .

2. They split the work in <u>half</u>. Each works on

_____

- - - - - - - - - - - - - - - - -

one of the _____ .

3. Giulio draws the pictures, and his <u>wife</u> writes the words. Many

_____

- - - - - - - - - - - - - - -

husbands and _____ work together.

4. Betsy and Giulio could each fill up a <u>shelf</u> with books of their own. But the books they have worked on together could fill up

_____

- - - - - - - - - - - - - - - - - - - -

many _____ .

5. Betsy and Giulio share a <u>life</u> of work. They are lucky to be able to

_____

- - - - - - - - - - - - - - -

spend their _____ together.

B. On another paper, write a sentence about your favorite story character.

NAME _____

Prefixes *re-*, *un-*

> **REMEMBER:** The prefix *re-* means "again" or "back."
> The prefix *un-* means "not."

A. Add *re-* or *un-* to make a new word.

turn

1. _____

draws

3. _____

wise

2. _____

writes

4. _____

B. Use each new word in Part A to finish the story.

Betsy and Giulio are very careful when they work on a book

_____

together. Betsy _____ her words until they

_____

are just right. Giulio _____ many of his

_____

pictures. They _____ to their work many

times to make sure that it is good. They know it would

_____

be _____ to publish a book that was not as

good as it could be.

C. On another paper, write two sentences about two people who

work together. Use one word with the prefix *re-* or *un-*.

Cause/Effect

> **REMEMBER:** Use signal words, story clues, and what you already know to figure out which events caused other events to happen.

A. Underline the part of the sentence that tells what made something else happen. Then write what happened.

1. Betsy loved children's books, so she became a kindergarten teacher.

_____
- -
_____

2. Giulio practiced and practiced, and therefore he became very good at drawing cartoon characters.

_____
- -
_____
- -
_____

3. Betsy began writing books for children when she met Giulio because she saw that he could draw wonderful pictures to go with her stories.

_____
- -
_____
- -
_____

B. On another paper, write a sentence that tells about something that happened to you when you tried hard to do something.

Characterization

> **REMEMBER:** To understand a character in a story, think about what the character says and does. Also think about how the character speaks and acts.

A. People like the Maestros make up many different kinds of story characters. Read what each of these make-believe characters says. Then write the word that tells what you think that character is like

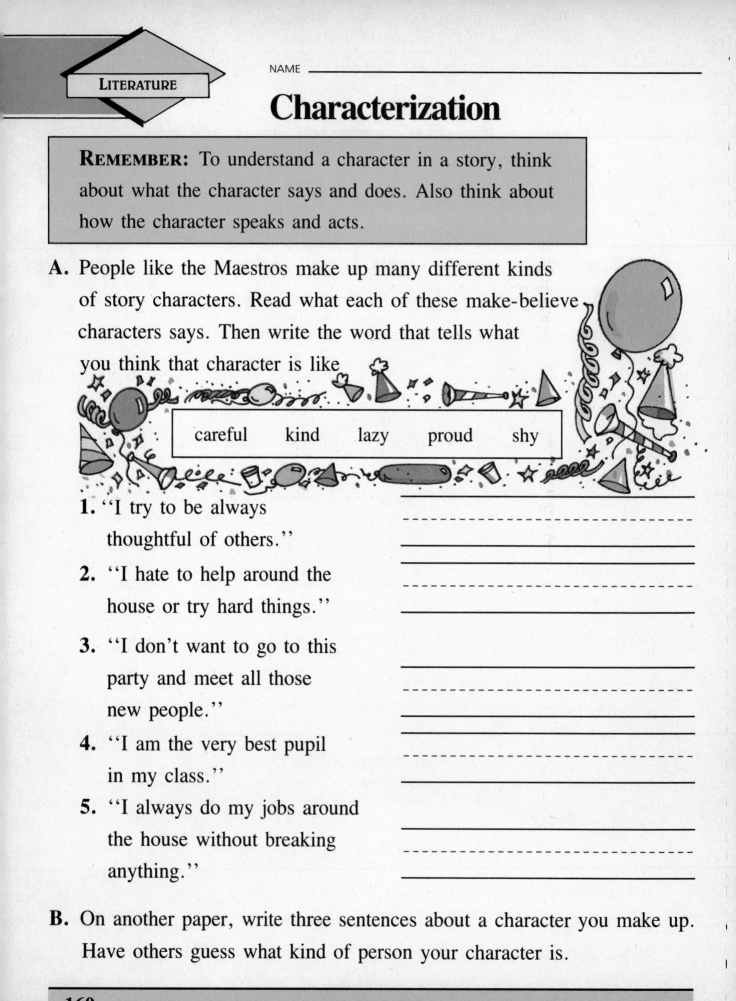

| careful | kind | lazy | proud | shy |

1. "I try to be always thoughtful of others."

_____

2. "I hate to help around the house or try hard things."

_____

3. "I don't want to go to this party and meet all those new people."

_____

4. "I am the very best pupil in my class."

_____

5. "I always do my jobs around the house without breaking anything."

_____

B. On another paper, write three sentences about a character you make up. Have others guess what kind of person your character is.

Synonyms

> **REMEMBER: Synonyms** are words that mean about the same thing. *Big* and *large* are synonyms.

A. Read each sentence. Then answer each question by writing one word from the sentence.

1. Betsy was very young when she discovered she loved books. What word means about the same as *found out*?

   _____

   _____

2. Giulio says that his work is like a hobby to him. What word means about the same as *job*?

   _____

   _____

3. When Betsy met Giulio, she began writing books for children. What word means about the same as *started*?

   _____

   _____

4. Giulio draws wonderful pictures to go with Betsy's stories. What word means about the same as *great*?

   _____

   _____

B. On another paper, write a sentence about your favorite book.

Checkpoint

Read the story. Then fill in the circle next to the correct answer.

Imagine living in a place that is cold all the time. People would need to wear heavy coats and scarves every day. There would be lots of snow. There would be no flowers or green leaves to enjoy. People would be unable to plant crops for food. They might even have to melt ice to get water!

Now think about life in a hot place. Try to imagine what life would be like. You would want to unbutton your heavy coat and unwrap your scarf! Each year you could replant crops for food, because many things grow in hot places. If you lived in a hot place all your life, you might not even know what snow looked like!

People live in many different places. Some live where it is very cold. Others live where it is always hot. People's lives are different because the places they live have different kinds of weather.

NAME _____

1. People who live in cold places cannot grow their food because ___.
   (a) crops will not grow in cold places
   (b) they have to wear heavy coats
   (c) they have to melt ice to get water

2. People's lives are different because ___.
   (a) some people live where it is cold
   (b) the places they live have different kinds of weather
   (c) some people live where it is hot

3. Which sentence tells something that living in a hot place could cause?
   (a) You would want to unbutton your heavy coat.
   (b) You might have to melt ice to get water.
   (c) There would be lots of snow.

4. What word belongs in this sentence from the story? People need to wear heavy coats and ___ every day.
   (a) scarf   (c) scarves
   (b) scarfs

5. What word meaning fits the underlined word in the sentence? People could replant crops.
   (a) not plant
   (b) plant again
   (c) full of plants

6. What word belongs in this sentence from the story? There would be no green ___ to enjoy in the spring.
   (a) leaves   (c) leave
   (b) leafs

7. What word meaning fits the underlined word in the sentence? You would want to unbutton your coat.
   (a) with buttons   (c) not button
   (b) button again

Vocabulary Review

Fill in the circle next to the word that best fits in the sentence.

1. The big ___ pulled the cart.
   (a) ox   (b) hotel   (c) statue   (d) strength

2. People liked to listen to Jill, who was a good ___ .
   (a) statue   (b) waiter   (c) fork   (d) talker

3. Fran ___ milk into her glass.
   (a) poured   (b) cleared   (c) promise   (d) published

4. Dick will ___ to clean his room.
   (a) ordered   (b) slid   (c) promise   (d) marry

5. Our park has a ___ of a man on a horse.
   (a) pizza   (b) yeast   (c) sawmill   (d) statue

6. Alan told funny ___ at the party.
   (a) utensils   (b) jokes   (c) talker   (d) wheat

7. Ricardo worked as a ___ in the restaurant.
   (a) waiter   (b) hotel   (c) journal   (d) statue

8. William ate his meat with a ___ and a knife.
(a) hotel   (b) fork   (c) journal   (d) waiter

9. Liz stayed in a ___ when she was away from home.
(a) characters   (b) statue   (c) hotel   (d) dough

10. My cousin Ed is going to ___ Kristin in June.
(a) marry   (b) weave   (c) breathe   (d) slid

11. A ___ is a place where you go to eat.
(a) waiter   (b) fork   (c) talker   (d) restaurant

12. Pat baked the ___ to make some bread.
(a) hotel   (b) ox   (c) dough   (d) fork

13. Anne kept a ___ of what she did every day.
(a) journal   (b) lumber   (c) restaurant   (d) dough

14. The two ___ cut down some trees in the forest.
(a) voyages   (b) cartoons   (c) routes   (d) loggers

15. Marc used ___ to make the table.
(a) ox   (b) lumber   (c) waiter   (d) statue

NAME _____

Unit Wrap-Up

Write the answer to each question.

1. Gus in "A Smooth Move" moved from Portland, Oregon, to Washington, D.C. Aiko, the mother in "How My Parents Learned to Eat," moved from Japan to the United States. Who had more to learn in the new place?

_____

_____

_____

_____

2. Think of the places you learned about in this unit. Which place would you like to visit? Why?

_____

_____

_____

_____

3. How can you learn about other places without going there yourself?

_____

_____

_____

_____

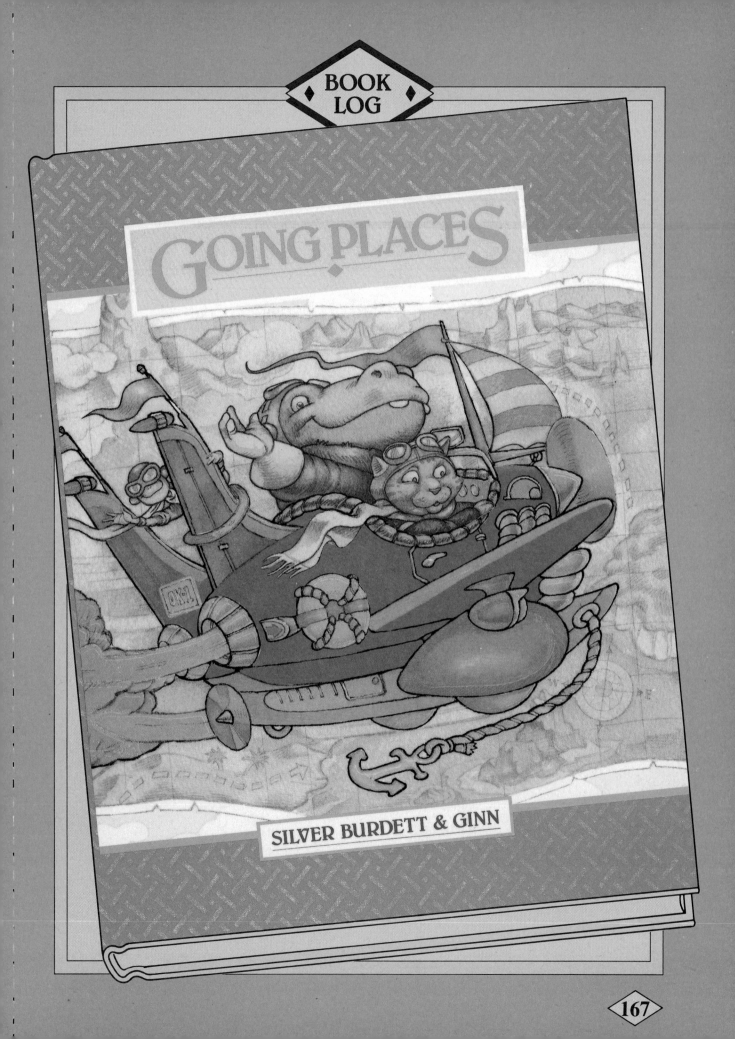

GOING PLACES

SILVER BURDETT & GINN

BOOK LOG

TITLE _____

AUTHOR _____

Here is a picture of something I learned.

How Many Stars?
Circle your answer.
★★★★ Super!!
★★★ Very Good
★★ O.K.
★ Not Good

NAME _____

BOOK LOG

TITLE _____

AUTHOR _____

THE STORY TAKES PLACE HERE.

THE IMPORTANT CHARACTERS ARE HERE.

How Many Stars?
Circle your answer.
☆☆☆☆ Super!!
☆☆☆ Very Good
☆☆ O.K.
☆ Not Good

NAME _____

Title _____

Author _____

Book LOG

Draw Your favorite Scene.

How Many Stars?
★★★★ Super!!
★★★ Very Good
★★ O.K.
★ Not GOOD
circle Your Answer.

NAME _____

MAKE A **BOOKMARK** FOR YOUR BOOK.

DRAW A **PICTURE** FROM THE BOOK.

WRITE A FEW **WORDS** THAT WILL REMIND YOU OF THE BOOK.

TITLE_____

AUTHOR_____

How Many Stars?
Circle your answer.
☆☆☆☆ Super!!
☆☆☆ Very Good
☆☆ O.K.
☆ Not Good

171

BOOK LOG

TITLE _____

AUTHOR _____

Here is a picture of something I learned.

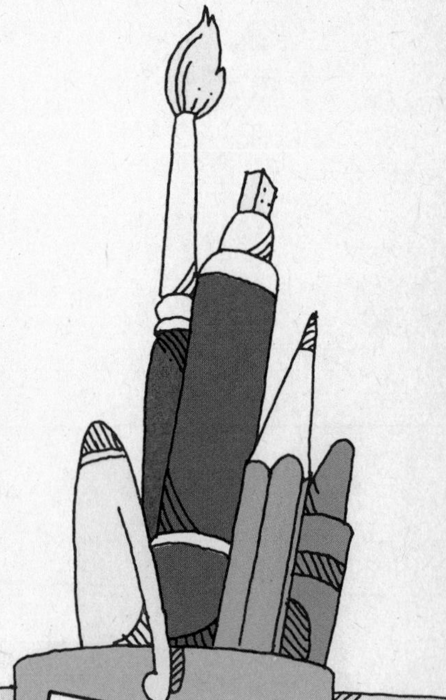

How Many Stars?
Circle your answer.
★★★★ Super!!
★★★ Very Good
★★ O.K.
★ Not Good

NAME _____

TITLE _____

AUTHOR _____

THE STORY TAKES PLACE HERE.

THE IMPORTANT CHARACTERS ARE HERE.

How Many Stars?
Circle your answer.
☆☆☆☆ Super!!
☆☆☆ Very Good
☆☆ O.K.
☆ Not Good

173

NAME _____

Title _____

Author _____

Book LOG

Draw your favorite Scene.

How Many Stars?
★★★★ Super!!
★★★ Very Good
★★ O.K.
★ Not GOOD
Circle your Answer.

174

NAME _____

MAKE A **BOOKMARK** FOR YOUR BOOK.

DRAW A **PICTURE** FROM THE BOOK.

WRITE A FEW **WORDS** THAT WILL REMIND YOU OF THE BOOK.

TITLE _____

AUTHOR _____

How Many Stars?
Circle your answer.
★★★★ Super!!
★★★ Very Good
★★ O.K.
★ Not Good

NAME _____

TITLE _____

AUTHOR _____

BOOK LOG

THE STORY TAKES PLACE HERE.

THE IMPORTANT CHARACTERS ARE HERE.

How Many Stars?
Circle your answer.
⭐⭐⭐⭐ Super!!
⭐⭐⭐ Very Good
⭐⭐ O.K.
⭐ Not Good

G H I J — W — 96 95 94 93 92 91 90